The Focal Dystonia Cure

Powerful and Definitive Practices to Completely Heal Yourself

Ruth S.L. Chiles

Attuned Press

Contents

Part Three

Practical Steps To Dissolve Your Focal Dystonia

Praise for The Focal Dystonia Cure

"I'd been struggling with focal dystonia for a very long time before I met Ruth Chiles. Her unique approach was exactly what I needed. Yes! There is hope for us all."

—Victor Wooten, Five-Time Grammy Award Winner

"Every word of Ruth's book hit home, as if it was meant for me. And if it's in your sights, I bet it's meant for you too. Having worked directly with Ruth in weekly Zoom sessions, I can verify, unsurprisingly, that she's done an exceptional job getting her process down on the page. After twenty years of trying just about everything, I finally understand exactly how my focal dystonia came about and exactly how to extinguish it. I am forever grateful.

"I can pretty much define my personal growth in two parts: before and after I encountered Ruth Chiles and her work. I came to her with two separate dystonic issues: one related to writing and another to playing banjo. She helped me kick the first, and we have the latter up against the ropes. But it's more than that. Along the way, she's turned me into a better human, which is far more important."

—Boo Walker, Bestselling Fiction Author

"Whether you are personally suffering from focal dystonia or whether you are a dedicated Brainspotting therapist, this book provides deep insights and effective step-by-step guidance in recovering from focal dystonia."

—David Grand, PhD, Founder and Developer of Brainspotting

"If you have focal dystonia and have come to this book looking for help, look no further—you've come to the right place. I've personally suffered from focal dystonia for over 15 years, and Ruth showed me how to find my playing and myself in record time. I've sought out help many times before from other focal dystonia gurus—that search stopped the moment I found Ruth. I have absolutely no doubt that she can help any focal dystonia sufferer. Ruth, from the bottom of my heart, thank you."

—Gonçalo de Oliveira Crespo, Guitarist and Music School Owner

"Ruth Chiles's deep understanding of focal dystonia and the recovery techniques that she offers have been nothing short of miraculous for me. As an artist and musician, I have gone from the terror and despair and disability of focal dystonia in my right hand to full recovery of my hand and my life."

—Audrey Bell, Artist and Guitarist

"Ruth Chiles knows what you're feeling and thinking. She's been there, having had focal dystonia herself, and she understands and has felt the guilt, shame, and fear that comes with it. Her book gives you a comprehensive process to understand the 'what' and 'why' of focal dystonia along with simple, powerful, self-guided exercises to resolve it.

"Ruth is a 'miracle worker.' She has an incredible ability to listen, perceive, and guide you to your own resolution of your focal dystonia. I wouldn't be where I am today without her and her method.

"You are not alone. If you're ready to resolve your focal dystonia, this is the path."

—David Ciucevich, Clarinettist, Multi-Instrumentalist, Operatic Tenor, Consulting Hypnotist, and Brainspotting Therapist

"I went from not being able to play a single note to, in about two months, being able to play for more than one hour on my horn and feeling great about it and finding pleasure in playing."

—Alain Tessier, Musician, French Horn Player

"I have resolved so much trauma causing inability to heal and even function healthily when it came to playing the violin. Because of Ruth, I am now in a neutral state, allowing me to play without physical strain."

—Joe Baca, Violinist with Mariachi Cobre, Composer, Educator

"Ruth's passion, compassion and unique perspective of having dealt with focal dystonia herself, gives her the ability to drill down to the root of dystonic symptoms. The exercises she has provided have helped me down the path to recovery from focal dystonia. It has been my absolute pleasure to have worked with her as a personal client."

—Paul Toutant, Trombonist and Educator

"This book gives a succinct description of Focal Dystonia, it's root causes and it's troubling manifestations in the body. Not only that, Ruth offers technical evidence-based exercises to help ease symptoms and return the system to homeostasis – a hugely valuable contribution"

—Georgina Hall, Brainspotting Therapist, Mindfulness Teacher, Artist

Ruth S. L. Chiles

Editing by The Pro Book Editor

Cover Design by Damonza

paperback ISBN: 9798427919036

1. SEL009000 SELF-HELP/Creativity
2. PSY020000 PSYCHOLOGY/Neuropsychology
3. SEL024000 SELF-HELP/Self-Management/Stress Management

UK English

First Edition

Para Levi, contigo mis sueños se hacen realidad

Foreword

In 2003 I discovered what I soon designated as Brainspotting. In the subsequent years, this approach evolved into a relational, brain-body mindfulness-based healing modality. Brainspotting guides its therapists to both attune to the client at the most profound level of human connection and to simultaneously follow their brain-body processes.

Nearly twenty years of Brainspotting evolution has revolutionised the practice of more than 15,000 therapists across the globe, with new trainees added every month. Beyond this, Brainspotting has transformed the lives of its recipient clients as they experience daily the remarkable healing that it potentiates.

Brainspotting has revealed its powerful effects in the performance arena, both sports and the arts. For years Ruth Chiles has been one of the noted pioneers in these fields. She has adapted and expanded my concepts on overcoming performance blocks and expanding performance and infused it with her over thirty years of experience. Ruth has simultaneously refined this approach with laser-like precision as well as broadened its scope.

In 2006 I met and subsequently worked with former New York Mets baseball catcher Mackey Sasser. Mackey's pro career was ended by a notorious case of throwing-back-to-the-pitcher yips. His problem was so publicised that his block was named as Sasser Syndrome and Mackey Sasseritis.

This career-ending performance block derived from both a complex history of sports injury traumas as well as significant childhood personal traumas. My successful work with Mackey is well documented in my book coauthored with Dr. Alan Goldberg, *This is Your Brain on Sports* and the ESPN documentary *Fields of Fear*.

The yips is well known in the sports world; however, athletes superstitiously avoid the term, referring to it as "the thing" or simply "it". However, it appears in other fields as well under different names, such as writer's block, stage fright and surgeon's shakes. Its medical designation is focal dystonia.

When I initially met Ruth Chiles, I knew she was a talented and dedicated Brainspotting therapist. I was, however, soon to learn that she was also a musician who had suffered from focal dystonia. She subsequently adapted all the Brainspotting that she learned from me and applied it to performance, especially the yips. Her personal journey of resolving her focal dystonia and returning to playing music has provided both the domain of focal dystonia and that of Brainspotting with invaluable insights.

As a scientist, Ruth has conducted significant research into how underlying traumas contribute to focal dystonia's impingement of neurophysiological fine motor skills and motor commands. Accordingly, her book provides in-depth phenomenological knowledge interwoven with sound scientific theory. Ruth has applied her irresistible passion to explicate the neuroscience of focal dystonia, it's aetiology and most significantly how to integrate and apply Brainspotting for successful treatment outcome.

This book provides an invaluable guide for musicians and athletes struggling with the deeply personal limitations of focal dystonia. For all therapists, Ruth elucidates crystal clarity on the fundamental skills of interoceptive sensitivity, self-regulation and coregulation. She also reveals how to expand your own self-attunement, an essential ingredient in your ability to attune to those who seek your help.

Whether you are personally suffering from focal dystonia or whether you are a dedicated Brainspotting therapist, this book provides deep insights and effective step-by-step guidance in recovering from focal dystonia.

—David Grand, PhD, Founder and Developer of Brainspotting

Introduction

This book, *The Focal Dystonia Cure*, is based on my experience with focal dystonia and the research I have done about its causes and treatment. The scientific studies that my research is based on are given throughout the book and include those on the physiological changes that occur in the brain that cause focal dystonia as well as on the natural techniques I use to reverse them. The method I have created from this research enables my student's body to work once again with complete control, harmony and fluidity.

Focal dystonia is a silent suffering that can be experienced by anyone but is most often diagnosed in athletes, musicians, dancers, writers and surgeons. It is often misdiagnosed, so the person suffering from it frequently has to try many different therapies before finally being correctly diagnosed.

Focal dystonia affects a muscle or group of muscles in a specific part of the body, thus the term *focal*. It causes undesired and involuntary muscular contraction, hyperextension or twisting and can affect many parts of the body, including the muscles of the eyes, mouth, vocal cords, neck, hands and feet.

Introduction

Highly precise movements become impossible to perform despite the person using all their concentration and effort. What makes it even more perplexing is that it often appears all of a sudden. Examples that I have worked with are musicians who can't maintain their embouchure (the way they use their lips, facial muscles, tongue, inner cavity of their mouth and teeth to direct the air into a wind instrument), their tongue is unable to create the beginning of a note, their fingers go into spasm and fold tightly into the palm of their hand or hyperextend outward, and sports people where an area of their body suddenly locks up and stops them from executing a movement or allow them to release the ball.

It is estimated that 1 percent of musicians suffer from focal dystonia, and up until now, there has been no truly effective treatment. Traditional treatments include Botox injections in the affected muscles with short-term results and risk of muscle damage. Muscle retraining is sometimes prescribed, though research has shown this treatment has a limited ability to resolve the suffering.

I began to play music at about four years old when I came across my brother's recorder. It was so much a part of my life that no one could extract the instrument from my hands. Music connected me to a whole new world and communicated to me in a way that gave me purpose like nothing else did. It was like a being able to speak a different language that transported me to unknown inner landscapes, feelings and experiences. It was like a magical gift that opened inside me dimensions and sensations that no other form of communication could.

I began my classical music education on the clarinet at ten years old, and at eighteen, almost overnight, I was unable to sustain my embouchure. The air leaked so strongly from the corners of my mouth that I could play no more. At that time there was no diagnosis of focal dystonia, and my teachers just told me I had to practice more. However, as much as I tried, I was unable to sustain my embouchure. I had to accept that I was unable to play any longer. It left me with a gaping hole in my life and a fascination about performance blocks, their causes, and most importantly, how to resolve them.

I intuitively knew what had caused my focal dystonia, as it had shown up in other areas of my relationship with music. For example, for a number of years before the onset of the dystonia, I suffered from stage fright, mental blanks and anxiety when practicing.

After I finished my university degree, I was employed by the then-largest bank in the UK to research and further develop my expertise in performance enhancement. They were wonderfully supportive in funding me to train and learn with the world's leading neuroscientists and psychologists. Later in my career, when I established my own consultancy, I focused my work more specifically towards athletes and musicians. It wasn't long before someone came to me with focal dystonia. By that time, I had healed my own embouchure dystonia and come back to playing music. My method proved to be precise and successful, and the news got around. Since then, I have dedicated my consultancy exclusively to focal dystonia.

I have now reached a point where my method has been consolidated and proven over many years, and I want to make it more widely available. That is my principal intention for writing this book.

The book is divided into three distinct parts. The first part explains the neuroscience of focal dystonia. The second part explains how and why these neurological changes occur. The final part of the book gives step-by-step exercises to follow that are designed to resolve these changes, therefore resolving your focal dystonia.

I share many real stories of my students so you can relate to the experiences we all have. It also gives a better and personal understanding of the possibilities that lie ahead for you. I have changed the names in each of these personal stories to respect their privacy.

I have made many references to musicians throughout the book. This is in part because I work most frequently with them. However, I have also used them as the focus of attention because the degree of fine motor skills they need to recover is much greater than for most people. Additionally, a partial recovery is insufficient for them. By including this degree of detail, this becomes a complete reference book for everyone who suffers from focal dystonia. The exercises are relevant for all people from all walks of life. I would go even further and say that anyone who suffers from chronic tension, anxiety, phobias or panic attacks will find many answers in this book.

The book is designed to be as highly practical as possible. It is also written to give you the maximum degree of personal empowerment in your recovery journey. However, sometimes working with a therapist is necessary, and the book's aim is not to replace the need for a specialist, nor for a complete medical diagnosis. I guide you in how to assess when you are able to work independently with the exercises I have written for you and when it is advisable to reach out for professional support.

To be able to resolve their focal dystonia, many people require an about turn 180° in the way they think about and understand it. The neuroscience that I explain in the book will give you a logical understanding of why this is. However, in addition, we need to engage deeper parts of our brain that are beyond logic. They are the parts that have a deeper way of comprehending things that can only be reached through metaphor. Therefore, as we come to the end of this introduction to the book, let us take a step into allegory in order to set the tone for our journey together.

Introduction

Close your eyes and imagine for a moment that you are in a relationship with someone who is profoundly important to you and with whom you share a home. Now feel what it would be like if this person paid no attention to who you are and what you need. Moreover, each time you try to communicate with them about it, they completely ignore you. Really take a moment to feel your reaction of what it would be like.

Can you imagine the impotency and frustration? Perhaps you feel like screaming at them, shaking them, or perhaps you just give up and become resigned to the situation.

What If....

What if this is exactly how your body feels towards you.

It would mean taking a 180° about turn towards how you have most likely been treating your focal dystonia. When they first contact me, most people have the attitude of wanting to make the dystonia go away. They have been trying to control or retrain their movements so they can regain control of their body once again. However, what if the dystonia is your body screaming at you because you have been ignoring it and its needs, probably for decades. Retraining and striving for control has just been a continuation of the same deaf-ear relationship you've had with your body.

This book is a scientific, experiential, metaphoric, and anecdotal journey towards deeply "listening" to what your body is trying to tell you through its dystonic movements. Along the way, I will explain what this means at a neuroscientific and experiential level; however, I am going to ask you to humour me a little longer with this allegory.

If we go back to the situation that we imagined earlier, how would it feel if the other person began to carefully listen to you? What would happen to your feelings of impotence and frustration? Would you need to continue to scream to make yourself heard?

Introduction

In this tone, I would like to share a poem by Rumi, a thirteenth-century Sufi poet.

The Guest House
Translated by Coleman Barks

This being human is a guest house.
Every morning a new arrival.

A joy, a depression, a meanness,
some momentary awareness comes
as an unexpected visitor.

Welcome and entertain them all!
Even if they're a crowd of sorrows,
who violently sweep your house
empty of its furniture,
still, treat each guest honourably.

He may be clearing you out
for some new delight.

The dark thought, the shame, the malice,
meet them at the door laughing,
and invite them in.

Be grateful for whoever comes,
because each has been sent
as a guide from beyond.

At the end of their process, once one of my student's dystonia had faded away, he—we'll call him Ray—looked intensely into my eyes, his eyes full of light as he said, "I realise that the dystonia was a gift. Perhaps the greatest gift that I have received. I hadn't realised how many negative mental habits I had developed. They just felt normal to me. It really did clear me out and sweep my house clean. I now feel free to enjoy life and my music in a completely new and wonderful way."

This and similar comments are the most frequent reflections I hear at the end of the process. So, in the time we spend together, we are going to treat your focal dystonia as an honoured guest, and we will meet it with joy and openness. We will listen deeply to its wisdom, knowing that it is truly a guide from beyond.

Part One

The Neurological Causes Of Your Focal Dystonia

Chapter One

Getting Down to the Roots

Your focal dystonia isn't just about the part of your body that is expressing these dystonic symptoms. There are much deeper-rooted issues to listen to and resolve. As we progress through the first part of the book, you will glean more of an understanding of these root causes, gaining a new mental framework to understand why your body is making these movements.

The number one priority for your brain is your survival. It will put this before everything else. In fact, below your conscious awareness, it is using your five senses to constantly scan everything going on around you for signs of safety or danger in a process called neuroception. Neuroscientists estimate that it is doing so at a rate of eleven million bits of perceptual information per second!

As a result of this constant monitoring, your nervous system will either be in safe mode or survival mode, depending on what your neuroception is noticing. Some people's nervous systems run most of the time in survival mode. There are various expressions of the survival mode of the nervous system.

You might relate to many of them, and it is also likely that they just feel normal. You may not even be aware that your nervous system is not in well-being, let alone realise other options are possible. You may be surprised at some of the descriptions and say to yourself, but I have been taught that being that way is highly valued and just what we are all striving towards. As you continue to read this book, you will instinctively comprehend how focal dystonia is not in your body, but it really reflects the survival mode of your nervous system. You will travel into an inner world where you experience how this mode forms a "dystonic mindset", patterns of thinking and behaving within you. I am using the word *dystonic* quite literally, "dis-tone", to be out of tune or mis-attuned and, therefore, not in harmony within you, nor with the world around you. From there, you will look out into our society to realise how dystonic our society is in its structures, values and expectations.

When our nervous system is in survival, it can either enter a hyperactivated or hypoactivated state. The foundation of focal dystonia is the long-term presence of either of these survival activations in the nervous system.

The Hyperactivated Nervous System

Hyperactivated means that it is activated above the normal level of activity. At its most extreme, it is readily recognisable because it is expressed as fear, anxiety, panic attacks, anger, frustration or rage. However, it can also be expressed in more subtle ways, which many of us have normalised as a natural and healthy way of being. You may even believe that it is who you are and part of your personality.

In the UK we have the phrase he "gets my back up". Close your eyes for a moment and think of those times when someone or something has irritated you. Feel the tenseness in your upper back as it lifts upwards. Perhaps you are aware of your muscles priming in your jaw, or perhaps they are more than primed and actually feel tense. You may also feel the same priming or tension moving through your scalp, neck, arms, hands and thighs.

As you continue to explore this state, ask yourself what your eyes feel like. Do you notice how they feel harsh or are staring? Notice how your breathing has shallowed and quickened and how your heart rate is elevated, even if it is subtle.

How do you feel towards the other person or situation? It is unlikely that you feel warm and connected to them. More than likely you feel separated, unfriendly and even distant from them.

Continue to feel these sensations so you can become more conscious of them. Notice how some of your responses are physical sensations like muscle tension or priming. Others are emotional, such as feeling a separation from another person, and others are mental, as you might have negative thoughts or distrust them. You might feel that someone or some people have treated you badly or that you are a victim of what they have done. You might feel justified in wishing them the worst. You may even feel justified in doing something against them in reaction to what they have done to you.

Once you have taken the time to become acutely aware of how your inner world was in this situation, also become conscious of what physical, mental or emotional sensations you carry around with you most of or all of the time.

In general, how do you feel towards other people? Do you feel warm towards them? Do you feel at one, connected and trusting? Perhaps your experience is the contrary. Perhaps you feel threatened by them, even if it is only slightly. Perhaps you feel like you have to compare yourself to them or have feelings of competitivity, superiority or inferiority towards them. Your feelings regarding others might be even stronger than this. You might feel that people can't be trusted and that you have to guard or protect yourself from them. You might even feel suspicious of others or bitter towards other people or life itself.

Your feelings may be more subtle. They may express themselves as disinterest towards other people. Perhaps you prefer to be on your own or just with a handful of very trustworthy friends.

On the whole, what is your mind like? Is it busy? Are you able to just be still and silent, or do you get fidgety and have to be busy or on the go all the time? Is your mind full of constant thoughts? Do you consistently analyse things in your mind, needing to understand and make sense of them? Perhaps your mind is so active that you just have difficulty focusing on or remembering things as they jump around like monkeys.

Alternatively, you may have hawk-like focus. It may be quick and agile, able to make sense of, understand things, and solve problems with great ease. This probably makes you feel good about yourself. You may well like to set objectives and never lose sight of the ball until your objectives are achieved. These objectives, plans and their execution fill your mind, and like a dog with a bone, you don't let go of thinking about them until you have made them happen. Having things ordered, tidy and structured is pleasing. It feels good to be in control and to be the master of your destiny! It feels great to create a high bar and reach it, to do things so well that other people notice or recognise you for it. It feels good to be seen and to take up time and space. It feels good to feel special, unique and important. When this happens, you can let go of striving, as you will finally feel that you are enough.

You may have a completely different experience. You may feel like life is chaotic and out of control. Does that make you feel like you need to escape or get away from the chaos?

Perhaps it makes you feel like you need to be in control of the circumstances with your plans, actions, goals and behaviours to avoid this chaos and uncertainty.

I have a list as long as my arm of the people I have helped who came to me with a hyperactivated nervous system. Jacob was a classic example.

A successful musician and businessman, Jacob was proud of his achievements, drive and focus. He set high goals and used his willpower to reach them. It was important for him to have everything under control. He had microscopic focus on every detail of his life, with a need to analyse and understand everything.

At the beginning of our work together, he had a challenging attitude towards me. He tried to put me on the spot, consistently questioning me and almost demanding that I justify myself and my methods.

In our early sessions, I explained to him that our aim was to retain all his great capacity for achievement. At the same time, it was to connect to the deeper parts of his brain that could enable him to achieve even more without tension and rigidity. I explained that we increase our choices and options if we can use more of our brain.

He began to understand that he needed to deactivate his level of drive, control and striving. At the beginning, this was a highly challenging idea for him. He soon realised that the achievement orientation and effort he was putting into the exercises I gave him was getting in the way. He began to understand experientially that the more he tried, the more the exercises evaded him.

The positive aspect of setting his sights high and his meticulousness meant that he was a diligent learner. He listened to me and allowed me to guide him. As I did so, he learned how to let go and drop into a calmer part of his nervous system. As he did so, he found that he had access to an inner intelligence that he couldn't have imagined he possessed.

In the process one of his most impactful realisations was how serious he had become. He became aware that he rarely laughed or had fun. He also discovered how this created deep-seated and underlying tension in his body.

During the months we worked together he made a beautiful transformation. He became joyful, playful, relaxed and open. With his newfound intelligence, he achieved more with less effort. As you may have guessed, another outcome of this transformation was that his hand dystonia also faded away.

The Hypoactivated Nervous System

The term *hypoactivated* means there is lower activity than normal. It begins with the feeling of wanting to retreat into yourself, like going inside a dark cave and disappearing. It is a need to escape the pressure that life puts on you. You just don't have the strength to face things, and as everything presses down on you, you may even find your energy drained away. Perhaps life has just exhausted you and left you spent of your strength.

People and situations might feel overwhelming, and you may have the feeling of just wanting to collapse. Perhaps you feel like you have a sea of tears inside and that you could cry for a whole year. You may feel small—or want to be small—and not take up space and time. You might feel transparent and even invisible. Perhaps you want to sink into the ground and disappear.

You may have an unheard, quivering voice inside calling out for someone to help you, to give you strength, to bolster you up, or even to come for you and take you away from it all. At the same time, you feel alone and separated from people. You feel the suffering and hostility of the world and how it has robbed you of your inner sun. You may have moments when the world feels like such a fundamentally unsafe place, and you may not want to be here any longer, or you might wish you can escape into death.

Nothing seems to make sense or have meaning any longer. Nothing captures your attention or fills you with motivation. Everything just seems grey and flat.

These final descriptions are those of a profound hypoactivated state in your nervous system. For you the sensations may not be this extreme. They may just be the beginnings of wanting to curl into yourself. Or you might notice that you have less energy, and things just seem a little greyer and two dimensional. You may find that these feelings are not constant or come in moments that then pass.

It is true that I see less people with a hypoactivated nervous system than hyperactivated; however, I have worked with some very memorable people who have come to me in this state.

For instance, from the moment we met, Michael struck me as a sensitive and creative soul. The experiences he had lived through left him feeling that the world was an aggressive and overwhelming place. He had withdrawn into a small life where he avoided engaging with others as much as he could.

As we worked together, I realised he was also significantly disengaged with himself. He found it difficult to connect with what his body felt and could only concentrate for short periods of time. He described how his brain would go into a fog, as though he disappeared into it. At the same time, he described how he felt like all his vital energy had disappeared. He only wanted to curl up and fall asleep. This was accompanied by the feeling of a frozen shell around his body. He would even touch his skin and say how cold it was.

As you might imagine, our initial sessions focused on building strength into his nervous system. In this way we enabled it to come back into a sense of safety. As we did so, he realised that his hand dystonia reflected this sense of frozenness and weakness in his body. As his nervous system strengthened and thawed out, so did his hand. In doing so he was able to gradually recover its strength and fluidity.

You may find yourself in situations where you are hyperactivated. Then in other moments or with certain stimuli or situations, you are thrown into hypoactivation. I have purposefully taken you into this self-exploration because when our nervous system is hyper or hypoactivated, we lose connection to ourselves and our inner world, especially in our bodies. We become what is called dissociated. This happens because the nervous system reads things in a black-and-white manner. We are either safe or under threat, and threat is equivalent to our lives being in danger. At this level of our brains, there are no subtle distinctions. It can't register a situation as just being a little uncomfortable because it reads everything that is not safe as life-threatening.

When your brain thinks it is in a life-threatening situation, it prepares and primes your body to be ready to flee, fight or become immobile. If you flee, your body wants to dissociate from any potential muscle fatigue or injury so you can run away at full speed until you are far enough away. If you fight, the dissociation occurs so you don't shy away from any pain the predator or attacker inflicts on you, which means you will keep fighting at full strength. If you become immobile, your brain has registered that neither of the other options are possible—you can't get away, and the predator is much stronger than you. It then makes you so still that the predator thinks you are already dead or doesn't see you and passes you by. This is the brain's last resort, so it is also preparing you for the worst-case scenario, which means that it creates the dissociation so you can be unaware of the pain of its mortal attack.

The result of this dissociation is that you are not aware of the physiological tension in your body, and that tension—along with the mental and emotional patterns—just feels normal. It is as though you disappear into this so-called normality and are unaware of who you truly are and what is happening inside you.

Chapter Two
Activation and Dystonic Movements

The activation of the nervous system leads to dystonic movements in your body. I have noticed that a convergence of three physical survival responses is in play. They are:

1. Dissociation.
2. The priming of large muscle groups.
3. The activation of primary survival movements.

As I explain each in more detail, see if you can feel like a row of dominos is falling. The last domino to fall is the manifestation of the dystonic movements in your body. It is valuable for you to get this sense because in the same way that it is the last domino to fall, it will probably be the last one to stand back up again.

In your recovery, we need to focus on putting all the previous dominos upright first. By this I mean that our focus needs come away from where you have the dystonic movements. We need first to centre on bringing your nervous system into safety, re-associating with your body and letting go of any ingrained dystonic mental patterns. As this happens, your body will automatically respond, and the dystonic movements will fade away on their own. Because of the way the brain automates movements and actions, the body may sometimes continue to express a little bit of the dystonia. This means that at the very end of the process when everything else is sufficiently resolved, we will, if necessary, focus on the physical body and pop upright the last domino.

1. Dissociation and the Loss of Interoceptive Sensitivity

At the end of the previous chapter, I talked about dissociation and how it is a natural and intelligent brain response. It protects you from danger and from feeling pain; however, if your nervous system has gone into survival mode, this dissociation becomes more pernicious. You lose connection to yourself, to others and to what is really going on inside of yourself mentally, emotionally and physically. This can have many negative consequences that include no longer feeling your physical body, passing your physical, mental and emotional limits, and staying in intolerable situations that continue to make your nervous system feel threatened.

One of the broader physical impacts of focal dystonia is that your dissociation has probably become extreme and focalised. Most people describe that they no longer feel in detail the part of their body where the dystonia has manifested itself, or that it is all they can feel. The people who have lost the feeling describe it as an internal map of that part of the body becoming muddled or blurred. Some people may feel as though that part of the body no longer belongs to them or that it is completely numb. On the other hand, people have said that the dystonic part of the body takes all their attention and they are constantly focused on it. The rest of the body feels like it has disappeared or gone to sleep. On a more general level, once they can feel their body, they often notice some asymmetry in it, meaning that one side of their body feels remarkably different from the other.

Another way of describing dissociation is the loss of **interoceptive sensitivity**. *Interoception* is a technical term that means the sense of the internal state of the body. It is both conscious and subconscious.

In practical terms, when we have a high level of interoceptive sensitivity, it gives us the feeling of really inhabiting the body and having a direct experience of how it feels from the inside. At the same time, we are aware of the emotional and mental tone accompanying the internal physical sensations. This is the direct opposite of the activated nervous system states. In these states we may be in our head and identifying strongly with our thoughts (meaning we believe that we are our thoughts, they are "who I am"). Alternatively, we may be outside of ourselves, somehow disconnected and absent.

A high level of interoceptive sensitivity is vital in our capacity to create and maintain homeostasis (internal balance and harmony in all our internal functions).

On a very practical level, interoceptive sensitivity is vital for us as musicians. The level of fine motor skills we require is so subtle and detailed that having a high level of interoceptive sensitivity is the base that enables this level of finesse in our technique.

In summary, the continued activation of the nervous system nulls our interoceptive sensitivity, creating dissociation and the inability for the brain to connect to and accurately govern and control certain areas of the body.

2. The Priming of Large Muscle Groups

It makes sense to realise that if our nervous system is in threat mode, it needs to ensure that we have the best chance of surviving the perceived danger. In simple terms, we need to be prepared to fight our way out of the situation, run and escape from it, or become immobile until it has passed. For each of these strategies, our fine motor skills are of little use. What the body needs is the power and strength of its large muscle groups.

In fact, whilst the nervous system is in survival mode, these large muscle groups are primed for action. We all know this instinctively because we have all had the experience of feeling tension in our shoulders when we feel stressed or worried. At the same time, the part of the brain that is responsible for fine motor skills is inhibited. Fine motor skills come from the intricate use of small muscle groups such as in the hands, tongue, lips and face.

Take a step back for a moment and consider the state of your nervous system when you are playing your musical instrument (be it during practice, your lessons or when you are performing). Are you goal orientated and obsessed with "getting it right", trying really hard and knowing that hard work is what it takes? Are you filled with self-talk about what you sound like and criticising what is not good enough about your playing? Do you compare yourself with others, or do you feel insecure about your technical abilities or threatened and insecure with your teacher, conductor, musical director or fellow musicians?

Perhaps you just have this sense of not being good enough yet, of wanting to perfect your playing and wanting to do so as quickly as possible. Sometimes you may have moments when you just think you will never get it, where you feel like you are out of your depth and an impostor, or where you just feel really uncomfortable and insecure. It may be that your goal is to play really fast and cleanly or hit those top notes like no one else can. You may even dream about being a world-class player that leaves everyone in awe. If any of these experiences ring true to you, it means that your nervous system is activated and in survival mode when you are playing.

In other words, when you are playing, your brain is inhibiting your fine motor skills and priming your large muscle groups. In this way, you are forcing your brain (probably for many hours each week) to create fine motor skills at the same time as inhibiting it from being able to do so.

This is like driving down the motorway in sixth gear and reverse at the same time! What do you expect will happen to the motor?

We are now getting a picture of how playing your instrument over so many hours with your nervous system in survival mode nulls your interoceptive sensitivity, disconnects you from feeling your body, and at the same time, forces your brain into forward and reverse. It is no surprise that this combination has a devasting effect on your fine motor skills.

3. Primary Survival Movements

Our body was born with six primary fine motor skill survival movements, as well as others that develop as we grow. The primary movements are instinctive and autonomous, and the brain knows how to perform them from birth. We didn't need to learn them, unlike all of our other movements, and they are not under the conscious control of us as babies. They happen automatically, in the same way that you blink and duck out of the way if something comes flying towards you. You are unable to control this response.

Two of these movements, the startle reflex and the suckling reflex, are particularly relevant to focal hand and focal embouchure dystonia.

The Startle Reflex

This has several aspects to it, one that is a hyperextension of the fingers followed by a hypercontraction of them (as they curl tightly into the palm of the hand). In babies, it is present so they automatically grasp on to the mother if they feel like they might fall. Whilst these two movements are often separated from each other in hand dystonia, they are equal to the primary survival movement of the hand. By this, I mean that some people just experience the hyperextension of the fingers, but other people experience just the hypercontraction. For other people, some fingers hyperextend whilst others hypercontract. I have even seen people who, before they worked with me, had experienced that the dystonia first appeared as a hyperextension and then changed over time to a hypercontraction, or vice versa. It is as if their hand got stuck in just part of the reflex.

The Suckling Reflex

This is a very complex movement. It involves the tongue moving towards the roof of the mouth as the muscles in the middle and back of the tongue harden. It then involves a backward movement of the tongue coordinated with the contraction and release of the muscles around the mouth, swallowing and breathing. I have seen over and over again how people with embouchure dystonia describe this exact movement happening whilst they are playing. This is the opposite movement from what we need when playing, which requires a soft tongue that moves forwards, upwards and downwards in the mouth, with just the tip becoming engaged to create precise articulation.

There are six other survival movements that we develop as we grow up, and they are also relevant to musician's focal dystonia, which are making a fist, snarling/smiling, biting, neck-locking and breath-holding. They also happen automatically and are not under our conscious control.

Making a Fist

When our nervous system is hyperactivated, one of its automatic movements is to prime the muscles in the shoulders, arms and hands to make a fist and be ready to strike a blow. I can remember how, when I was young, I would wake up to find my hands in a fist. Sometimes during the day, I would suddenly realise that my hands were curled into a fist. Whilst, often, we do have some conscious control over relaxing the hand, for many people the underlying subtle priming of the muscles do not relax as much as they try to make it do so.

Snarling/Smiling

Another of our automated responses is to snarl or smile. They come from the same fundamental movement and come out as one or the other, depending on the situation. If our deep brain perceives that we are safest if we create conciliation, it will create the smile movement. If it perceives that we need to show we are the aggressor to manage the situation, it will create the snarl movement. They use almost the same muscles, with just some subtle differences. Since we have been educated not to snarl in public, this movement usually comes out as a forced smile. However, the basic tensing and backward movement of the cheek muscles happens before we have had time to control them.

Biting

The third muscle group that becomes automatically primed is those around the jaw, which prepare the body to bite. As you increase your interoceptive sensitivity, you may well become aware of how much tension you constantly carry in your jaw. Most people who suffer from focal dystonia, be it embouchure or hand dystonia, hold significant tension in their jaw.

Neck-Locking

Neck tension seems to be one of the most epidemic experiences of people today. In a large part, it is caused by one of our defence reflexes. If we were out in the wild and there was a physical threat, such as a predator, our deep brain needs to keep it in sight at all times. It has this need because at light-speed velocity, it needs to assess the danger that this predator poses. For instance, you want to know if it is at a safe distance, if it has seen you, or if it is about to attack you, and so on.

To keep the danger in sight, the neck becomes locked in its direction to override the fear reaction that wants to look away and hide. At a simple physiological level, neck tension often leads to problems in the cervical vertebra, trapped nerves, and a difficulty for the impulses from your brain to reach, particularly your hands.

Throat-Tightening

In a similar way that the neck locks to overcome the fear reaction of looking away, the deep brain will sometimes tighten the throat and supress a scream response. Remember that as human beings, we naturally live in communities. The scream is an instinctive response to call for help or a warning to the rest of the community.

However, if the deep brain perceives that the best survival strategy is to remain unseen, it will override the scream response by tightening the throat. The most common way people describe this is saying they feel like they have a lump in their throat, they can't swallow, or that they feel like they have a rope or hand around their throat.

Breath-Holding

Last, but certainly not least, breath-holding is an automated and integral part of the hypoactivated state in the nervous system, as I talked about in the previous chapter. The survival strategy of the hypoactivation is to make the body as still and unperceivable as possible. It does this by tightening all the muscles to immobilise the body, creating a sense of inner collapse and a mental retreat into your inner world to disconnect from what is going on outside.

As part of this process, it needs to reduce the movements that our body makes. In order to do so, we breathe at an absolute minimum. Therefore, the muscles tighten to inhibit our ability to take a deep breath, making it as shallow and invisible as possible. This is why so many people with focal dystonia describe how their breath seems to get stuck in their body or feels blocked in some way.

The key issue about these responses is that they are not under our conscious control because our survival mechanisms are a priority for the brain. As I said earlier, the primary function of the brain, which comes before everything else, is to ensure our survival. Therefore, it uses the quickest and most powerful part of the brain to create these movements. I mentioned in chapter 1 that the deep brain, the part of the brain that is constantly scanning the environment (neuroception) for signs of threat or safety, works at a speed of eleven million bits of perceptual information per second. It is also working at this same speed in its response to a perceived threat. This part of the brain is our subconscious, meaning that it is below our conscious awareness.

The new part of our brain, referred to as the neocortex, does all our thinking. When we purposefully make a body movement, this is the part of the brain we are using. For instance, if I tell my thumb to curl into the palm of my hand, consciously making this movement, it is my neocortex that initiates the signal to move. Likewise, if I consciously try to relax my thumb, I am also using my neocortex to send that message. Whilst the deep brain, as I have mentioned, is estimated by the neuroscientists to work at eleven million bits of perceptual information per second, they calculate that the neocortex only functions at ten to sixty bits. That is a million times slower! Timothy Wilson's book *Strangers to Ourselves* gives detailed information on the various investigations that have led to these calculations of the processing power of the neocortex versus the subcortex of the brain.

Now you can understand why you are unable to think your way into making your body stop the dystonic movements. The thinking brain is simply unable to override the instinctive survival mechanisms of the body. It is just not fast or powerful enough to do so.

This realisation can be quite a shock to many people. After all, we have been brought up in a culture that values our thinking capacity beyond anything else. In René Descartes's words, "I think, therefore I am". We are a culture that has taken this statement and idolised the neocortex as the master of our brain and our life, who has ignored the value of what is going on in the invisibility of our subconscious and has not wanted to admit how much is occurring below our conscious control. Iain McGilchrist in his book *The Master and his Emissary* wonderfully describes many of the negative consequences of this erroneous approach.

If we add this all together, the dystonic symptoms begin to make sense. There is the dissociation with the body and concurrent lack of interoceptive sensitivity. You are asking your body to be in sixth gear and reverse at the same time as you play with your fine motor skills being inhibited. Then we have the automated survival movements of the body. A light begins to shine on why your body has become locked into these strange movements and why you are unable to control them no matter how hard you try.

Part 2 will contain the last piece of the puzzle regarding what causes focal dystonia. This is important to understand before exploring how to resolve the dystonic movements. It is the vital question: what has caused your nervous system to get stuck in this activated state?

Before we answer that, I would like you to have a practical tool to begin your recovery in the next chapter, the Attunement Repair Exercise.

Chapter Three
Stage 1 - The Attunement Repair Exercise

This is a highly practical exercise that is designed to give you many different benefits. The first is to repair and increase your interoceptive sensitivity, as I have already talked about. I will refer to the other benefits throughout the book.

Some people find this exercise easy, enjoyable and deeply connecting to do. I hope that you do too. However, it is also true that for people who have developed a long-term dissociative relationship with their physical body, the exercise can be very challenging. Remember that this dissociation is a natural response to the continued survival mode and its hyper- or hypoactivation in your nervous system.

If this is the case for you, I would like you to be really compassionate with and caring towards yourself. It is not that something is wrong with you or that you are not doing it right, nor is it that you don't know how to do it. It is just that the level of activation in your nervous system is too high for you to access the exercise. Therefore, if you find it too difficult to connect with this exercise, or if it is too activating for you to do so, reach out for support. You would benefit from accompaniment in some one-to-one focal dystonia cure sessions to deactivate your nervous system. Through my website (focaldystoniacure.com), you can contact therapists who I have personally trained and continue to supervise.

Even so, I still wholeheartedly encourage you to practice the exercise each day. This is because, by simply doing the best you can with it and with constancy, you will begin to connect with yourself and master the exercise a little bit at a time.

It is important that you don't confuse this exercise with guided relaxation exercises. It is distinctly different. Our objective is not to relax the body, mind or emotions, although some people do find the exercise very relaxing. Our objective is to come back into inhabiting the body just the way that it is. It is to feel the body from the inside with all its tensions, contractions, oppressions, openness, relaxation and freedom. It is to feel it just the way it is, without trying to change anything. One of the common human experiences is to grasp on to what feels pleasant and push away what feels painful or uncomfortable. However, if we come back to the very beginning of this book and Rumi's beautiful poem, "The Guest House", we want to welcome in everything just as it is. This means that as you practice the exercise, you are also practicing how to be in a still presence with everything that you feel equally—the pleasant sensations and the unpleasant ones.

As we get ready to begin the exercise, find a time and place where you feel comfortable and won't be disturbed for about twenty minutes. You might like to record yourself reading the exercise so the first times you do it, you can just lie back and follow the guided instructions. You may even wish to listen to the video that I have recorded guiding you through it. You can find it on my website (focaldystoniacure.com). Once you become practiced and experienced with it and can feel into it well, you may prefer to go through it without any guidance. This opens you up to more opportunity to follow your own inner wisdom and intuition and go at your own pace. Do what feels best for you!

You can do the exercise sitting or lying down, and as stated, you can do each part of it when you are ready. Many people at the beginning find it easiest to do it lying down, either on their bed, on a sofa or even on the floor on a yoga mat or a rug.

You will start by bringing your attention to your feet. Put equal attention into both feet simultaneously. You want to really inhabit your feet and feel them from the inside. Go inside them as a direct sensory experience of everything that is there right now, in this moment. This is an exercise of inhabiting with complete self-acceptance, so whatever you find there right now is perfect for right now. It may be different from yesterday, and tomorrow it may be different again, but we are in the here and now, so just feel into being inside.

Be present with being inside your feet, just as they are. Include every detail of the direct experience that you are having right now. You might become aware of the surface level of the feeling, then there is also the inside feeling. As you continue to do this exercise over the weeks and months, you will become more aware of all the details of how your feet feel on the inside. You may even feel and distinguish your skin, your bones, your muscles, your ligaments, your tendons, blood vessels, nerve endings, and so on.

If you are unable to feel this level of detail yet, that is also perfect for your right now. Accept your experience just as it is.

When you feel ready, you are going to slowly move up to include your ankles as well. So come inside your ankles and be completely present with the direct experience of them, just the way they are. Be present to all the details that you find there, from the inside out. Be aware of the three-dimensional experience of being inside your feet and your ankles.

Take all the time you need here, and only when you feel ready, you are going to move up to include your lower legs, your calves, your shins, the inside of the lower leg and the outside. Once again, having this three-dimensional experience, go right into the centre of your lower legs and your ankles and your feet. Inhabit them. Be present inside them, just the way they are right now, with everything that you find. Include, with gentleness, everything that is there.

Some people find it very difficult to connect with their body in this way, and they find that it helps to move the parts of the body that they are feeling into. Others find that they can have a feeling of filling their body up, starting with their feet, as though they are filling it up with a warm liquid. It helps them to start to have a sense of the three-dimensionality of their body.

Take all the time you need and only go as far as you can. We can take all the time in the world with this exercise. It is important to do it regularly, preferably daily, and allow yourself the time—be it days, weeks or even months—to connect with your physical body in this integrated way.

If and when you feel you are ready to continue, include your knees as well. The fronts of your knees, the backs of your knees, the inside leg parts of your knees and the outside and feeling right into the centre, into the three dimensions of your knees. Add that awareness and presence to the direct experience of your feet, your ankles and your lower legs. Your intention is to place your attention equally on both sides of your body, feeling the left foot, lower leg and knee with equal awareness as the right.

If and when you feel ready, you are going to continue up to your thighs, feeling your right and left thigh simultaneously and with equal awareness. If you are unable to do so, if one side of your body feels more present than the other, accept this gently as your experience right now and feel what it feels like. There is no need to change it, just be present to what you feel in just the way that you feel it. There are no right or wrong feelings or sensations with this exercise. We are practicing to feel what is there, just as it is and accepting it just as it is. It is the guest that we are welcoming into our house with an open heart and willingness to listen to it, even if its message is discomfort.

Add your experience of your thighs to everything else that you are feeling. Once again open yourself to it being a three-dimensional direct experience of being completely present and inhabiting your body. Do so on the surface level and right down into the centre.

I purposely say to open yourself to the experience. There is no trying that you need to do here. Just let go and drop into whatever is there. Trying to do this exercise is like trying to remember a name. The more you try, the more it eludes you. It is when you let go of trying that the name spontaneously pops into your brain.

If and when you are ready, bring your attention up to your pelvic area and here—as well as muscles, tendons, ligaments, blood vessels, nerves and bones—you begin to find your organs. So as you add onto this experience and the whole of your pelvic area, be aware of it all, or as much of it as you can be.

Sometimes, we also find that we have blanks, or areas of the body that we have no access to feeling. If that's the case, that is also fine. It is your experience right now, the experience that you are including. Over time, as you practice this exercise, you will find that those blanks start to be filled in, and you begin to gain access to the physical experiences of being inside this area of your body too. So just for now, if you do find any blanks anywhere, as we continue this exercise, just let them be and experience them as part of your experience in the here and now.

Just take your time and continue to include everything up until now. Feel with equal awareness, if you can, the left and right side of your body at the same time.

You may find you can feel the bones of your hips, and from there move your attention inwards to fill up the whole of your pelvic bowl. That's it!

If and when you are ready, continue moving up your body, adding your experience of your lower back, your abdomen and the sides of your body at this level—the surface experience and the inner experience. You may even find that you can experience the sense of your spinal column and how it runs right down into your pelvic area, right down to your coccyx.

Take your time to feel into and be completely present in this part of your body, just as it is. Feel what you find, just as you find it, whether your experience is pleasant, comfortable or uncomfortable.

When and if you are ready, you are going to move up into your middle and upper back, your rib cage, sides and front, your sternum, your collar bones, shoulders and shoulder blades, and then feel inside to your diaphragm, your heart and your lungs. Include this experience and inhabit this area of your body as well, just the way it is. If there are areas or sensations that are less comfortable, include them too. Invite them with gentleness to be part of who you are and include them, just the way they are.

When you are ready, come into your shoulder joints and upper arms. Here, there are triceps on the back and biceps on the front, as well as the inside and outside arm. Feel right into the centre of this three-dimensional experience coming into, being right inside, and experiencing your body from the inside. That's it!

Add this to your awareness of all the other parts of your body that you have already visited and be present with them at the same time.

Include your elbows when you are ready. Remember, there is an inside and outside part of your elbows. Then include your lower arms, your wrists, your hands and your fingers. You might even become aware that your fingers run right up through your hands on the inside. The fingers go straight up to your wrists.

Feel everything together. Feel the whole of your body, everything you are aware of, to this point. With this latest part, as you become aware of your lower arms, wrists and hands, feel with equal awareness, if you can, the left and right sides of your body simultaneously.

When you are ready, we are going to include your neck. This includes the sides of your neck, the back of your neck and your throat. You want to be present inside your neck, throat, spinal column, and the muscles and soft tissue you can feel. Inhabit it, just the way it is, with whatever you find. All is welcome here, with this gentle awareness and presence.

There we go!

Now include your head, scalp and cranium into your awareness. Feel into your brain and brainstem as it runs up from your spinal column. You may even become aware of your entire spinal column and the whole of your central nervous system running from your brainstem and to your coccyx. You may or may not be aware of it, but it's there.

Then come up and feel all of your brain, including the lower part, the middle, top, front, and right into the centre. Feel it all at once with the rest of your body. As you do that, you will also include the rest of your face, forehead, eyes and eye sockets, the roof of your mouth, and your nose, along with the outside and inside parts of your nose. Then include your cheeks, your jaw, your chin, the outsides and insides of your ears, your mouth—the inside of your cheeks, the roof of your mouth, your teeth and gums, the floor of your mouth and your tongue. You may feel where your tongue begins right at the back where your throat turns into your mouth. Feel your lips, where they touch your teeth, as well as the outside of them. Feel your jaw from the joint, where it joins to your scull, and along the whole length of the jaw on the right and left to your chin.

Keep your entire presence inside this direct experience of your body. Focus on the left and right with equal attention, if that is possible. That's it! Just spend the time that you desire here, attuned to yourself and all the physical parts that are you and the way they are. Let yourself be just the way you are, accepting everything that you find. Nothing needs to change. Everything is just right and just as it is in the here and now.

When you are ready to come back, you can slowly begin to move your fingers and your toes. You can even make circles with your hands and feet, first in one direction and then in the other. If you want to stretch, do it, and be aware of your breath. You might take several deep breaths.

Gradually become more aware of the space around of you, the room you're in, and the sounds and temperature. When you're ready, slowly open your eyes and come back into the here and now. If you are lying down, slowly sit up. Move with gentleness, and as you move, remain aware of how your body feels on the inside. Gradually become aware of the world around you, maintaining the same level of connection to and awareness of your body. Include the world around you as you continue to inhabit your body and look out of your eyes, hear through your ears, and feel through your skin into this connection with yourself. That's it. Welcome back!

I recommend that you find some time to do this exercise every day. It is one of the most powerful ways of being more attuned to yourself. Remember, this is one of the critical and key parts of your focal dystonia resolution. Of all the people I have worked with, those who do this exercise daily and joyfully are the ones who progress most quickly and smoothly to a full dystonia resolution. As they look back on their process, they find it to have been the best investment of their time.

I hope you enjoy this exercise and that it brings you comprehension and connection to yourself.

Part Two

How You Became Locked Into Survival Mode

Chapter Four

Lack of Childhood Parental Attunement

I n part 2, you will learn the primary causes of activation in your nervous system. I will explain what happened to you that caused your nervous system to become locked into survival mode.

We can think of the causes in four groups, but you may have had experiences from just one of these groups. That is enough to have caused the survival mode activation in your nervous system and its physical expression into focal dystonia. However, I usually find that people with focal dystonia have had experiences in more than one group. Most people find that they feel intimately related to many of the experiences I am going to talk about in this chapter.

The four groups are:

1. A lack of childhood parental attunement.
2. Having been brought up in or having learned in the Oppression Model.
3. Adverse events.

4. All injuries, whether or not they are related to
playing your instrument.

In this chapter I will talk more about the first of these
groups—lack of childhood parental attunement.

Our primordial survival need as children is to feel that the
adults caring for us are attuned to us.

I hope that by now, you are beginning to have the experience of feeling attuned to yourself. Through practicing the
Attunement Repair Exercise, you may have started to feel
warmth and comfort from simply being present to yourself, just
the way you are, without expectations or criticism. This is
simply through connecting with and feeling who and how
you are.

It is like, as a child, coming into the warmth after having
been out playing in the snow. Oh, that deep comfort of being
wrapped up in blankets, as the cutting coldness melts away and
the rosy heat flows into the centre of your body. At the same
time, it seeps into your fingers and toes, bringing them back to
tingly life. You become filled with the glow of home, hearth and
holding.

In an ideal world, we would all have felt this degree of
holding, connection and attunement when we were children.
Ideally, the adults around us would have connected to us,
sensed who we were and what we needed, and they would
have responded to our needs with kindness, acceptance and
firmness. They would have offered us softness when we needed
it; guidance, discipline and direction when necessary and play-
fulness and fun just in the right measure. They would have
sensed our needs and responded with intelligence and love.

The key person for us as babies and in early childhood is
our mother. Before you were born, you shared a forty-week in
utero experience with her. This means that, by the time you

were born, you were not only biologically and genetically connected to her, but you were also connected historically, emotionally, psychologically and spiritually.

There is a continuity between this in-uterine and postnatal psychological bonding that we experience. This means that you remained psychologically merged with your mother for several months after you were born. During this time, you still felt contained within your mother, so whilst you were no longer physically inside your mother's body, your sense of self was psychologically enveloped within your mother's self. It is what Eric Neumann calls the "extra-uterine embryonic phase". It is a gradual process that occurs throughout the first year of life when you flowed into a state of having your own sense of self, separate from your mother. Ideally it would have been an uninterrupted continuum where you would have been maintained in a sense of wholeness and rightness of self, with trust in the continuity and the goodness and rightness of life.

Donald Winnicott has provided us with much of the subtle understanding of this process. He describes how although the baby and mother are separated physiologically at birth, they are psychologically, emotionally and spiritually still one. They are mother/baby, one unit, where there is no such thing as baby.

We can no longer assume that babies are unaware and unfeeling, as all the research that has been completed clearly indicates otherwise. Babies feel on physical, psychological, emotional and spiritual levels.

A very large proportion of people who later suffered from focal dystonia had an early attachment break with their mother. This may have happened because they were born prematurely, because of illness—be it their own or that of their mother— because of adoption or because their mother was unable to attune to them.

If this was your story, you may feel—within your body—the

impact of the sudden absence of the person to whom you were connected and expected to welcome you into the world. Imagine how bewildering and terrifying it was for you to be handed over to a complete stranger to take care of you. Moreover, handed to a stranger that has no physical, hormonal, psychological nor emotional connection with you to mirror or feel your needs. That stranger could have been a nurse or nurses, a foster parent, other family members or even an incubator.

What's more, at this age, a baby's brain does not have a developed hippocampus, which is the part of the brain that gives you a sense of time. So, a baby separated from its mother, even if only for an hour, has a sense that this separation has lasted an eternity. It feels like it has died, or like it is dead but alive. This type of collapse into the realms of death happens inside, as if part of them has fallen into a place of continued grey, concrete, drizzling sadness where their sense of wholeness has been annihilated. Here there is no sun or colour, no plants or animals, and no bright sound of birdsong or pealing laughter of children. There is just empty, imploded grey silence.

It is as though there is a deep, embedded sense that in a moment of crisis or survival, you might be forgotten or left out of the circle of protection because the instinctive thread that creates it, without thought in a moment of pure reaction, is lacking.

Let me explain. When I was a child, I spent most of my weekends playing at my friend's sheep farm. In the spring we would help her father with the lambing season. He would tell us the importance of the initial and immediate bond that would occur between the mother sheep and her lamb. This occurred in the moments of its birth and the crucial minutes that followed it. He explained how it was the most vital part of the survival instinct. This invisible bond ensured the lamb was in the constant attention of its mother to provide it with milk, warmth, and to protect it from predators.

Many years later, whilst on holiday in Ireland, I saw this played out again. We were driving down a remote and leafy country lane in the early evening, just as the sun's rays became watery. Suddenly, in a gap through the trees, I saw a small herd of deer. We stopped the car and crept as close as we could to see them without scaring them. They were beautiful. There were three female deer and a fawn. Whilst we had been stealth-like and maintained our distance, the mother's instinct was finely honed. In the moment that she perceived our presence, she placed herself in front of her fawn to hide it from our view. Within seconds the other does had also surrounded it to give it their full protection.

Without this connecting thread, an infant is left with the most primitive sense of being unprotected. They have no feeling of being held in this instinctive maternal presence. They lack the felt-sense of this all-embracing presence of their mother, which is like the universal heart of safety and well-being. It is a place of complete relaxation, where alertness can be switched off and all is well. In fact, the lack of this thread feels like terrified eternal helplessness, lack of food or shelter, and impending death from a predator.

If I go back to my experience on the sheep farm, a lamb who is separated from its mother at the moment of birth is afterwards not recognised by its mother, and it does not recognise her. It becomes like an orphan; motherless, undefended, lost, just because of those few instants of separation in that most critical of moments. We would need to raise these lambs by hand, keeping them indoors and bottle-feeding them. They never seemed to completely release their sense of lostness and confusion.

Our brain is constructed from our early experiences. They

form the structure of our neural networks, where every new experience becomes built on and connected to previous ones. These initial life experiences are aptly called formative experiences, as they are like the pillars and beams of a house. They form the key foundational structures where the whole house will be built, upon which the whole structure of the neural networks of the brain will be formed.

A deep-seated survival fear and hyperalertness is created if our initial experience is disconnection from the mother/baby unit that gives us our sense of self and bonding. In addition, we will sense that part of us—or at least something—is missing. This is one of the supporting beams that all our future experiences will be built. It becomes the filter of sorts that everything else passes. Everything becomes distorted through its tint and remembered in relation to it.

Even though new bonds can later be created with our mother or other members of the family, they are like speaking a second language, never quite having the fluidity and naturalness of our mother tongue. Knowing what connection feels like isn't in our consciousness. How can you even know that something exists when you have never experienced it? So even when there are healthy connecting moments afterwards, it is like they are, albeit partially, filtered out and can't get fully in to be felt, registered and recognised for what they are. The inner vocabulary of connection seems to be lacking or just doesn't exist. Oftentimes, no matter how much or how often the child is shown or told he or she is loved, they are unable to fully believe it.

Therefore, we need to give ourselves the permission to fully acknowledge and mourn our losses. Only then can they surface from the dark depths of our psyche where they will otherwise lurk as a shadow which keeps us from experiencing joy. If they stay in the darkness, they will continue to cause the crippling feelings and behaviours that have become so familiar. In fact, they may be so familiar that they are just the way life is and just the way you are; however, this is not true. These feelings and behaviours are natural responses to the primal grief that has no voice and that were your earliest experience of life. They are feelings that come from events that we cannot consciously remember, yet we can intuitively feel inside of ourselves. When we give ourselves permission to validate our intuitive inner world as true, we give ourselves the possibility to heal what otherwise just feels like devastating confusion.

Frequently, I work with people who tell me that they have had no difficult experiences in their life. However, as I describe the sensations as I have done so in this chapter, they feel like they can completely relate to them. Sometimes they even feel the dark-cloaked shadows of these sensations rise inside of them. It seems like they had been lurking in the shadows, desperately waiting for someone to realise they are there.

This reminds me of Richard, who attended one of my masterclasses. Throughout the class he was sure that nothing untoward had happened to him in his life. However, at the same time, he recognised that his nervous system had been hyperactivated for as long as he could remember.

When I spoke about early maternal attachment breaks, I saw how my description rippled through his body like an earthquake. He felt it too, which left him perplexed. On the final day of class, he admitted that he had been born prematurely because his mother had suffered health problems towards the end of the pregnancy. However, he still didn't feel convinced that this could have affected him so strongly.

After the class, he wrote to me and said that he had been asking his parents about his birth and the early days of his life. Unknown to him, up until that point, his story was much more complex. Not only had he been born prematurely, but his mother was strongly affected by the birth and her health difficulties. So much so, that during the first six months of his life, she was unable to pick him up, feed him, or take care of him in any way.

His grandparents lived a long way away, and his father worked full time. He was left in his cot without any visual, physical or emotional contact from his mother, nor anyone else, for many hours every day.

At the end of his note to me, he said that so many things were beginning to fall into place. He told me that he was finally understanding why he had been plagued his whole life with difficult feelings, thoughts and sensations that had never made sense to him.

This means that even if you believe that you have not had any of the experiences I talk about in this and the following chapters, don't ignore your inner knowing. If deep inside you feel connected to my words or your body and mind respond to them as if they are yours, trust in your reaction.

It is all too common that we have had experiences that no one has told us about. Oftentimes, our family feels embarrassed about the events and never tells us about them, or they change the story for it to be more acceptable or comfortable. Therefore, it is important that we learn to trust in the interoceptive sensitivity we are developing. It really doesn't matter whether you ever come to know the whole story. If your body or intuition connect to inner sensations that are similar or related to those that I describe, listen to them. Open up to them being real. Trust in the truth of them and give them space inside of you. Dedicate them the time they need for you to feel and connect with as much of the subtle details of your inner world as possible.

As we continue our journey, I will describe how you can heal your personal story. For now, there are two key steps that will begin to heal you. The first one is simply recognising yourself in what I have described in the previous paragraphs. The second one occurs as you permit yourself, as I have described, to connect with and give validity to the intuitive or physical sensations you have in relation to it. It would be very valuable to be especially aware of and caring towards them whilst you are doing the Attunement Repair Exercise.

I started this section talking about early maternal attachment breaks, because their impact is so foundational and therefore profound for the brain. However, not everyone who later develops focal dystonia has lived through such a break. For some people it was more of an ongoing general lack of attunement that they experienced throughout their childhood.

This lack of attunement can have many forms. It may be from both parents, or it may be from just your mother or father. Given that there are so many forms of it, I will talk about it in general terms.

At the beginning of this section, I talked about what it feels like as we attune to ourselves. This is what it would have felt like if your parents had skilfully attuned to you when you were a child.

If they had been good at attuning to you, they would have had enough time and inner silence to feel and comprehend what was going on in your inner world at any given moment.

Bear in mind that the human brain does not become fully developed until between twenty-five to thirty years old. Before that time, it lacks many adult capacities. Much of our childhood would ideally have been spent having just the right stimuli to create our optimal brain development. One of the key stimuli is the attunement that we receive from the adults around us. Our parents are particularly important, as it is with them that we have our strongest natural bond. It is possible for us to develop very healthy attachments with other adult caring figures. However, our initial and natural bond is with our parents.

Let me explain more about the relevant cerebral capacities, in relation to focal dystonia, that we lack as children and how parental attunement helps us develop them. They are:

1. Our capacity to regulate our emotions and be able to calm ourselves.
2. Our verbal abilities, meaning that we have a limited ability to talk about what has happened and what is going on inside of us.
3. Our capacity for self-attunement.

Attunement and Emotional Regulation.

Very small children haven't developed the capacity to sooth themselves when they feel upset and are unable to regulate their emotions. If they get upset, angry, sad, frustrated, scared, overexcited and so on, they become completely taken over by the emotion and are unable to manage it. They need an adult to calmly connect with them. If this adult is calm and silent on the inside, they can just be present with the child. As they do so, they "tune into" him or her and can comprehend what they are feeling. The effect on the child is that it begins to calm down and feel better.

Let me explain what is happening in the brain of both the adult and the child. In the centre of our brain, we have what is called our limbic system. Sometimes it is called the mammalian brain. It is in this part of our brain that our deep emotional states arise. In the past twenty-five years, there has been significant research completed on how our limbic systems synchronise with the people we interact with. This idea was written about by Thomas Lewis, MD, Fari Amini, MD and Richard

Lannon, MD, in their book *A General Theory of Love*, which was published in the year 2000.

In this book they shared three key ideas:

1. Limbic resonance: our brain chemistry and nervous systems are measurably affected by those closest to us.
2. Limbic regulation: our systems synchronise with one another in a way that establishes our lifelong emotional tone in our personality.
3. Limbic revision: if we did not establish healthy patterns in our childhood, they can be positively modified through therapy.

Two other important researchers in this area are: Dr. Allan Schore, of the UCLA David Geffen School of Medicine in his book *Affect Regulation and the Origin of the Self*, and Dr. James Coan, associate professor of Clinical Psychology and Director of the Virginia Affective Neuroscience Laboratory at the University of Virginia. His study is called "Why we Hold Hands".

These researchers, as well as others, have shown that our limbic systems synchronise with each other. It is a bit like when you put two wine glasses close together. If you dampen your finger and run it around the rim of one of them, it will vibrate and make a musical note. The glass that is next to it will also vibrate at the same time and make the same note, seemingly all on its own.

Through the limbic resonance, we can feel and sense what another person is feeling on the inside. This was important to us as children because we hadn't yet developed the ability to describe our feelings in words. Particularly when we were very small, we were unable to verbalise what was happening to us on the inside. If we had parents who were able to attune to us, they were able to sense, through their limbic resonance, what was going on for us and respond appropriately.

Children who have grown up in such an environment receive several benefits, including:

- They have a deep sense of being understood and of being safely "held".
- They intrinsically know that their feelings and experiences are valid, and they feel validated as a person.
- As they grow up, they learn how to self-regulate their emotions. They do so through their experience of strong emotions being calmed down through the calm presence of the adults around them (this is called coregulation).

When we lack adult attunement, on the other hand, we grow up with a very different sense of self.

Earlier in this section, I talked about how our sense of physical safety depends on knowing that our adult caring figures are attuned to us. We need to instinctively know that we are constantly in their awareness to know that we will be fed, taken care of and protected in the face of danger. I also mentioned in an earlier chapter that the primary task of our nervous system is to ensure our survival. This means that if the person who cared for you daily wasn't attuned to you, you needed to attune to them. You constantly needed to disconnect from your needs and experiences to connect to those of your carer. You did so, unconsciously, to keep yourself present in their attention. Remember how we talked about dissociation in chapter 2? For many of us, this is where our dissociative movement began.

If this was the case for you, it is likely to have installed several sensations in your sense of self:

- Your needs, feelings and sense of self don't feel valid or important. This may lead you to either dismiss them completely or to no longer feel them. On the other hand, it may have had the opposite effect, where you are constantly searching to be seen, receive attention and be validated by others. You particularly search for it from people who are important to you or who are authority figures.
- You have a deep, gnawing sense of not doing enough or just not being enough. It is almost as if a very young part of you believes that if only you were better, different or had done better your parents would have attuned to you.
- You probably had to deal on your own with the difficult experiences you went through as a child— conflicts with friends, bullying, or even the doubts and questions that childhood and adolescence naturally bring. This meant that these and even everyday difficulties probably became more strongly impacted in your nervous system than they would have if you had been able to share them. I will talk more about what I mean by this on the section about adverse events.
- As we mentioned in chapter 1, this left your nervous system in a state of hyper- or hypoactivation.
- As a result, you may notice that you are more sensitive than other people and find it more difficult to self-regulate your emotions. You may feel a dependence on others to feel safe or calm.

For many of us in childhood, we not only experienced a lack of attunement, but we received ongoing mis-attunement from the adults around us. This may have come in the form of harshness towards us or dismissal of our feelings and experiences. It may have been in the form of criticism or humiliation. At its worse, it takes the form of ongoing psychological, emotional and/or physical violence and neglect. These experiences have a devastatingly negative effect on our brain, nervous system and sense of self and relationship with the world.

Chapter Five
Upbringing or Learning in the Oppression Model

To define what I mean by the Oppression Model, it is first useful to have an overview of how we use our brain when we learn and play music. This is just a simple description as I don't want to bog you down and lose the thread of what is important.

We can divide the brain in half from top to bottom. On the top we have the neocortex. This is the new part of our brain. It is the part that enables us to have conscious thoughts and awareness. It is extremely useful in making sense of and categorising things. As I mentioned before, neuroscientists estimate that it functions at the amazing speed of ten to sixty bits of perceptual information per second. The neocortex is involved in higher functions such as sensory perception, generation of motor commands, spatial reasoning, conscious thought and language.

Underneath it sits the subcortex, *sub* meaning underneath. This is the centre of our subconscious. This means that everything that occurs in this part of our brain is below our conscious awareness.

The subcortex is responsible for motor control and skills learning (in the basal ganglia). It is also responsible, in the limbic system, for the detection and expression of emotions. They can be fear and threat emotions (using the amygdala), laughter (in the hippocampus) and positive feelings (through the connection between the amygdala, thalamus and hippocampus). The hippocampus also plays an important role in learning, memory and detecting novelty. The other main function in learning of the subcortex, in the thalamus and hypothalamus, is to receive sensory information from the senses of taste, hearing, sight and touch. The hypothalamus also regulates body temperature, hunger, sexual behaviour and thirst.

If the neocortex works at the amazing speed of ten to sixty bits of sensory information per second, the subcortex is mind blowing at its around eleven million bits of perceptual information per second.

Let's pause here for a moment to reflect on the famous phrase "Cogito ergo sum", of the seventeenth-century French philosopher René Descartes, that I mentioned before. It is usually translated as and understood as meaning "I think, therefore I am". When we begin to understand the functions and power of the subcortex, which is doing everything in our subconscious, we can realise that, perhaps, this idea has taken us down the wrong path. We can realise that it would be more accurate to turn this phrase on its head to read "I am, therefore I think".

Whilst it is true that the thinking part of our brain (the neocortex) gives motor commands and makes sense of things, such as music theory, it is not the part of the brain that plays music. It just works too slowly to do so.

It is our subcortex, the part of our brain that we are not consciously aware of, that learns and executes the fine motor movements necessary to have the necessary technical finesse. It is the subcortex that hears the sounds we are creating and has the tactile feedback necessary to adjust our fine motor movements to express the sound that we wish to communicate. If this wasn't enough, it is the subcortex that experiences and expresses the emotions that are the central power and meaning of music.

When we reflect on everything that is occurring on the inside when we create music, it seems strikingly obvious that it requires the brain speed of the subcortex, and the ten to sixty bits of information of the neocortex is just too sluggish to be of much use.

Since we have had this moment to reflect on the amazing way your brain functions, I will define the Oppression Model in relation to learning. The simplest definition is the insistence on performing or learning subcortical functions using the neocortex. It feels controlling, rigid, serious and harsh because the neocortex, as we have just seen, simply does not have the capacity or speed to perform nor learn these functions. It feels like hammering a square peg into a round hole to force it to fit. It feels frustrating and damages our self-confidence because we believe that our lack of progression is because we are just not good enough.

As I continue to describe the experience of the Oppression Model in more detail, my aim is for you to recognise it in yourself and your education. I would also like you to understand the negative impact it has had on you.

Let me start with the undercurrent that drives the Oppression Model. Have you ever swum in a river or the sea when there is a strong undercurrent? You can't see it from the surface, but as hard as you try to swim where you desire to go, it drags you from underneath. It is exhausting and often impossible to fight against. The undercurrent of the Oppression Model is just like this. Moreover, many people have grown up with it from such a young age that it just feels normal and they don't even resist its pull. In fact, they even swim with it, not knowing that it is taking them far away from what they truly desire.

The undercurrent I am referring to is an often unconscious need to be recognised as being brilliant, a genius, and better than others. It is fed by a false belief that there is personal value in being so. That by being a better musician than my peers, I am intrinsically more valuable than them and have a higher self-worth. It is nourished by a foundational sense of identity of not being enough.

I talked in the previous section about some of the most common reasons why this feeling becomes installed as a deep identity trait. I call it an identity trait because it goes far beyond believing oneself to not be "good enough at...". It is a sense that simply who I am as a human being is not enough and that "I will only be enough if I achieve...".

In this belief, we constantly look for external recognition of our achievements. Therefore, we look for our measure of worth, particularly from authority figures or people, we have put on a pedestal.

Perhaps one of the gifts of focal dystonia is that it strips away the false object of our sense of worth. It leaves us totally barren in relation to this prop. This is one of the reasons why it feels totally devastating. For many musicians, one of their initial reactions is to feel that their life is over. As we journey through this book, I will show you how to release this false belief. You will learn how to deepen into knowing that you are enough just as you are. You will feel your value as a human being and how it has nothing to do with what you achieve. It is a strange conundrum of life, that as we sink into this new and true sense of identity, we are set free to become and realise our full potential. It is through no longer needing to stand out or receive recognition that our true brilliance shines at its brightest.

However, until this time, we become stuck in the Oppression Model. Here, our sense of self-worth is intrinsically linked to our sense of survival. This is because at our most instinctive level, we are a "pack animal", where those who are higher up in the hierarchy have first access to food, shelter and to reproduce. Therefore, if we have a low sense of self-worth, we instinctively feel at risk of going without.

Whilst we, of course, have a much higher awareness and attributes as well, this instinct sits there under the surface as a survival issue. This means that unless we learn to engage this higher awareness, it will subconsciously drive our emotions, thinking and behaviour. If it becomes expressed into the Oppression Model, we become driven by the need to control results and outcomes. Our subcortex becomes obsessed with the control that it falsely believes is necessary to "keep us safe".

We set ourselves often unachievable goals with timescales for achieving them. We become unyieldingly fixed on achieving these goals exactly as we have set them. We become driven, rigid and analytical in our attempts to control these outcomes. Our motivation is extrinsically orientated—if I do well, I will be recognised and valued. The other side of this coin is the fear of making mistakes and not reaching the bar and the deep dark hole of worthlessness that we falsely believe this means. Like a sharp winter frost, we harshly focus on our mistakes and what is not good enough, rather than allowing the springtime of enjoying, praising and celebrating our small advances. In the narrow channels of our minds, we are not good enough until we have reached the level of perfectionism or virtuosity that we have imprinted there. We relentlessly drive ourselves to practice for hours and hours with furrowed-brow concentration, serious, often micro-obsessed, and analysing just one detail of our playing. We are not allowed to relax and feel satisfied until we have gotten it just perfect. Have you found yourself going over and over the same phrase, lick or note using your will power, concentration and control to dominate it? In this Model we are constantly comparing ourselves to others with our internal critic vociferously looking at everything down to its microscopic detail.

When we learn technical skills on the instrument, it is done so from an external focus. By this I mean, we are told what hand position to have, how to form our embouchure, or how to control our breath. We are rarely guided to feel inside our body to use our interoceptive sensitivity. In the Oppression Model, we are told what to do rather than being encouraged to use our curiosity to explore interoceptively what the technique feels like on the inside and to hear the sound it creates.

The Oppression Model leads us to believe that the goal is to "get it right" rather than to learn, explore and make mistakes. Many of us have a fear or even terror of making mistakes. We think so much in terms of right and wrong that we are trying to get it right all of the time. We might feel awful on the inside if we make a mistake and go over and over it in our mind afterwards as we struggle with feelings of shame and embarrassment.

In summary, there are several key themes in the Oppression Model:

- It sets big goals or expectations and tells us that we are not good enough or have little merit until we reach them. It does this rather than highlighting the next small and easily achievable step in your progress. It is pressured and serious rather than allowing us to explore, enjoy, be playful and take our little steps.

- It focuses on the outcome, rather than a solid interoceptively sensitive method that will naturally lead to it. It is always under time pressure, compressing the sense of time and space to achieve the outcome as soon as possible. It is as if the uncertainty of how your playing will improve over time is too uncomfortable to bear.
- It confuses your creative and technical abilities with your self-worth.
- It is critical, judgemental, competitive and compares you to others in terms of better and worse. Errors or when you fall short of the bar are treated with judgement, your playing being termed as good or bad. There is a lack of neutral understanding of what is causing the sound to be the way it is and what to do and practice to improve it.
- Practice is done through obsession and hyperfocus. It is done through "trying" and using your neocortex to control your movements. It is based on a rigid sense of discipline and obligation. It doesn't understand that an intelligent understanding of discipline is to be constant and yet relaxed and playful in relation to your practice.
- It requires long and forced practice, that does not listen to your emotional, mental and physical messages of tiredness or pain. It has a no pain, no gain attitude. It fails to realise that working smart is much more effective than working hard.
- It does not provide an environment where it is safe to explore and make mistakes. All too often mistakes are publicly called out, shamed and even lead to humiliation.

- There is an external measure for what is right and wrong, good and bad, and the student's inner expression and interpretation are not validated.

The Liberation Model takes us to a different paradigm. At its most simple, it is when you can engage in an activity in safe mode. You feel attuned to the people and circumstances that are involved, and you feel that they are attuned to you. In addition, however, it also has some specific aspects that are important to highlight:

- It recognises the genius of your subcortex and encourages you to trust in all your innate abilities. It knows that we are all a fountain of infinite creativity and capacity waiting for us to build the skills to enable it to flood out.
- It welcomes all your experiences, capacities and abilities with kindness and understanding.
- It encourages you to deepen into and trust yourself and your interoceptive sensitivity.
- Learning happens through your subcortex, through feeling deeply into your interoceptive sensitivity. In this way, it is curious and playful. It does so without interference from your neocortex, without demanding, time pressures nor expectations of outcomes.

Sometimes, because of our feelings of not being enough, we impose the Oppression Model on ourselves. In other cases, we learned it through our family, school or musical education. In these circumstances, we find ourselves willingly swimming with the oppression undercurrent. In other situations, the Model is imposed on us by our family, teachers, educational institution, or teaching method. In this case, as hard as we try to swim in another direction, it drags us along with it.

Let's take another pause for reflection. First of all, think of a time when you were relaxed and having fun, laughing with friends, perhaps, and simply enjoying the moment. Go back there, as if you are there again right now. See what you were seeing—the faces of the people who were there and what was surrounding you. Hear what you were hearing, such as the conversations, the laughter, and perhaps even music playing. Feel how you were feeling, like the fun, lightness and relaxation. Attune into your body. How does it feel when you are relaxed and having fun? What does your mind feel like? Notice the lightness and spaciousness that it has. Take time to feel into as much of this experience as you are able to. Feel into every subtle detail. Use your improving interoceptive sensitivity to intimately connect with the direct experience of these sensations, on the inside. Take all the time in the world to enjoy and savour the experience.

When you are ready, slowly come back to the here and now. You might find that some of these lovely feelings come back with you. Look around and listen to the sounds that are surrounding you right now to make sure you are fully back.

When you are ready, let's have another different experience. Reflect on my description of the Oppression Model. What aspects of it can you relate to?

Take yourself to a moment when you were in your experience of the Oppression Model. Go there as if you are in it again. See what you were seeing. What surrounded you and who else was there. Hear what you were hearing. What was being said, and was music playing? Feel how you felt. What emotions are you feeling? How does your body feel? Where do you feel physical tension? What does your mind feel like? Is it light, open and clear? Or is it dense, constricted and heavy?

How does it differ from the first reflection, or an enjoyable moment?

This gives you a direct experience of the impact that the Oppression Model has on your physical body, mental clarity and capacity. It creates physical tension in the large muscle groups, most frequently in the shoulders, upper arms, forearms, neck and legs. It creates tension and gripping in the hands and toes. In the face, it often creates tension in the jaw, gums, teeth and tongue. There is tension in the lips and cheeks, and if you feel it closely, you will notice that it feels like they are pulling backwards. The other most common impact on the body is the breath and throat feeling restricted.

You will also have noted the impact that it has on your mind. You might even feel the physical tension in your brain. Even if you are not aware of this, you will notice the lack of clarity and mental denseness. People often describe feelings of mental fogginess, confusion and an inability to think as clearly and freely as at other times.

Take a moment to reflect on how this affects your coordination and speed of response. You will notice how the combination of mental and physical tension in your large muscle groups and in the areas of fine motor skills (be it your hands, embouchure or breath) make your movements sluggish, uncoordinated and even clumsy.

The most clear and direct example regarding the physical impact of the Oppression Model that I have worked with was José.

José had learned classical guitar from early childhood. He adored playing it and had learned in a warm and encouraging environment. His playing was fluid, exciting and widely recognised as being technically excellent. In his early twenties, he became inspired to study baroque music and its guitar-related instruments, such as the lute, baroque guitar, vihuela and mandolin.

He achieved a place in a European conservatory to study a degree in baroque music playing these instruments. Unfortunately, the teaching method was an extreme form of the Oppression Model. He and his fellow students were constantly berated for the angle of their hand on the instrument and the way they used their fingers to pluck the strings.

They were put under tremendous time pressure to change the whole technique they had learned on the modern guitar. They were expected to learn the new hand positions and finger movements that were required for each instrument in a very short time. In this time frame, they were expected to play and perform baroque pieces of music perfectly. In addition, they were expected to do so on various instruments, each one requiring a unique technique.

Our basal ganglia, the part of the subcortex that controls motor movement, also automate those movements. If you think about a baby when it learns to speak, it has to think about each sound and then each word. Over time, we only think about the overall message that we want to say, and all the individual sounds and words come out automatically. There are many similarities with learning and playing music. When we first learn, we are aware of each note we play. Over time, our basal ganglia automate the movements of the most frequent combination of notes. This frees us to centre on the overall expression of the whole phrase.

José's teachers did not give him the time that was necessary for his subcortex to interoceptively feel the new hand positions and movements on each of the instruments. Neither did they give his subcortex enough time to repeat those feelings until they became automated.

Therefore, when asked to play pieces of music al tempo, his

basal ganglia naturally went back to his modern guitar auto-mated movements. Each time, his technique was less than perfect, and each time, it went to his previously learned, auto-mated guitar movements. His teachers publicly reprimanded him.

You can imagine how his self-esteem and his confidence as a musician plummeted over the three years of studying his degree. You can also probably feel how much he had to use his neocortex to try to control his movements and how much mental and physical tension he developed in his body. By now, you have probably guessed that by the time he finished this degree, he had developed focal hand dystonia.

Sadly, José's story is not an isolated one. A too-large percentage of the people I have worked with and helped to fully recover from their focal dystonia have similar stories. Many people develop it as they are studying for their music degree, masters or doctorate. One of the key causes is the Oppression Model they are in or imposing on themselves.

You can see that when your thinking self (your neocortex) tries to take control of your learning process and of your play-ing, it puts you in the Oppression Model. In this section, you have seen how this undercurrent drags you in the opposite direction from where you desire to go.

Chapter Six
Adverse Events

This is the third category of circumstances that may have affected your nervous system, locking it into survival mode.

I would like to start by defining what an adverse event is. Then I will explain how it is related to trauma.

An adverse event is any event that you have experienced where you didn't have the resources to resolve it in the moment that it occurred. These resources can be:

- Physical, such as physical strength, money, transport.
- Emotional, such as having the emotional capacity to withstand the event without becoming blocked.
- Mental, having the mental capacity to resolve it, or to know just the right thing to say.

In reality, the term adverse event is synonymous to a traumatic event. I prefer the word *adverse* because I think that it is easier to understand and relate to. Many people think of a traumatic event as something violent or dramatic. They will often say that they haven't experienced any trauma. However, the truth is that anything we have experienced where we didn't have the physical, emotional or mental resources to face it has a trauma impact on our nervous system.

Therefore, as you begin to reflect on all the times you have experienced adverse events in your life, you can begin to realise the importance of these words.

An adverse event can be one-off or a continuous, prolonged or repeated situation. This means that it might have been something that just happened one time and then it was over. On the other hand, if it is a continuous situation, it is something that continued to occur repeatedly across a period of time.

If we studied in a music school, conservatory or with a teacher who taught us within the Oppression Model, this would be an example of a continuous adverse event. If we were brought up in an environment where there was a lack of attunement or active mis-attunement (for example in the case of emotional, mental or physical abuse or with a parent who was an addict) this is also an example of a continuous adverse event. Another frequent example of a continuous adverse event is having experienced ongoing bullying at school, in the workplace or in a musical group.

Continuous adverse events leave the person with a sense of being trapped, and the trauma becomes particularly embedded in the nervous system. This is particularly potent in locking it into a "permanent" state of hypo- or hyperactivation.

When I suggest the link between adverse events and focal dystonia, many people find it too big a leap to see the connection. I have already described in chapter 2 the physical consequences of the nervous system being hyper- or hypoactivated. Since we have explored the fundamental aspects of how our brain works in relation to our fine motor skills, let us explore the connection further.

A 2015 study by the Amen Clinic, published in *PLOS One*, explored SPECT scans of people who had experienced diverse forms of adverse events. They showed hyperactivity in various regions of the brain. The most significant alterations were in the following areas. Look at just how relevant they are to us:

- **The basal ganglia:** As we previously described, this is the area of the limbic system that is responsible for executing and automating our motor actions. It also helps in establishing the level of anxiety in the body. It is involved when we jump when we are startled, when we tremble because we are nervous, and when our body and mind freeze through fear. The study showed how the hyperactivation in this region of the brain is associated with an increase in anxiety, fear and tension in the body.
- **The amygdala:** The study showed how people who had suffered adverse events had an increase of activity in the amygdala, resulting in higher levels of anguish and anxiety.
- **Anterior cingulate cortex (ACC):** This is found in the deep part of the frontal lobe of the brain and works in close collaboration with the amygdala. You can think of it like the gear box of the brain, which allows you to shift from one thought to another or from having your attention on one area or another, or from one behaviour to another and so on. The study showed that in people who experienced adverse events, the

hyperactivity in this area led to them becoming stuck in one thought, one area of attention or in one preoccupation. They also tended to be more rigid in their thinking.

- **Thalamus:** As we saw previously, this is involved in processing the information that is received through the senses and in experiencing positive feelings. The study showed how this ability became modified, distorting the ability to effectively receive sensory information.

I was very inspired by this study, as it showed definitively how the brain responds to adverse events and gives a scientific explanation of what I was seeing phenomenologically in my work. This was not just in the physical body, but also in the dystonic mindset that I had already mentioned. It shows how it is inextricably linked with the manifestation of the body in the form of the dystonic movements.

For practical reasons, I have separated the causes of activation of the nervous system into four groups. These are a lack of childhood parental attunement, having been brought up in or having learned in the Oppression Model, adverse events, and all injuries. In truth we could term all four of them as adverse events. I have separated them into these groups because the lack of attunement, the Oppression Model and injuries have a very specific relevance in the formation of dystonic movements. Therefore, it is important to look at each one of them individually.

Perhaps what is most important here is to focus on the good news! The impact of adverse events on the brain is completely reversible. We will talk about how to do so in part 3 of the book.

Reflection 1.

Let's take a moment for reflection. Think about someone, a

group of people, or a situation in which you felt relaxed, happy, supported and understood. This could be a situation where you felt you could be yourself and express yourself freely or perhaps where you simply felt "at home".

If you are unable to think of an example, just skip this reflection and go straight on to reflection 2.

If you can think of one, imagine that you are there again right now. Close your eyes and think of who is there. Focus on their faces and look around to see your surroundings. Listen to the sounds that are around you. They may be voices and conversations, or they may be other sounds. Feel what it feels like to be there and to feel safe. What does it feel like in your physical body? What does it feel like mentally? What does it feel like emotionally? Take all the time that you fancy. Stay here for as long as you wish. When you are ready, slowly open your eyes and come back into the here and now.

Reflection 2.

Reflect on all the people and situations in your life when you didn't feel safe. Perhaps in some of them you were able to easily walk away, say what needed to be said or do what needed to be done to change it. If this was the case, feel how empowering it was. However, in others, you will find that you were unable to leave the situation. Reflect on your past to your childhood and how it felt to be in a situation or around people who make you feel unsure, uncomfortable or bad on the inside. There is no need to feel too deeply. Feel just enough to recognise the impact that such a situation had on you, when you didn't have the capacity or ability to change it, leave it, or make it stop. Each one of these situations is an adverse event that you have experienced in your life. There may be others as well that you do not consciously remember.

I have described what neuroscientific studies have demonstrated to be the impact of these events on your brain. However,

I also wanted to describe what it looks like, phenomenologically, when I am working with someone to help them resolve this impact.

It seems that adverse events become stuck in the brain. It is as if the memories of the event (be it one-off or continuous) are stuck in a capsule. It appears that it hasn't been integrated fluidly in the brain in the same way that other memories have been. Therefore, rather than existing in the past, it is still strongly present in the here and now. By this, I mean that when the person I am working with connects to the event, they can still clearly feel the emotions they felt back then. They sometimes have very nitid images of the event. Some might be still images, but sometimes it is a full film of what happened or parts of what happened. Their body also remembers the event in a very detailed way. Its reactions might not always make logical sense, but they will be there. For example, they may feel a knot in their throat, anxiety in their stomach, tension in their shoulders, an accelerated heart rate, and tightening in their muscles. The list is endless, and each person's response is unique. Frequently, the mind also reacts, as they notice a change in their thinking.

Usually, the event doesn't exist on its own in the capsule. As we open it, a flood of events emerges. Many of them don't seem to have a logical relationship to each other. Here, we are engaged with the subcortex, which exists below our logic. Here we come to realise that the brain has its own way of understanding the relationship between our different life experiences.

Your brain is truly amazing. It is a miracle!

Your brain is predisposed to wellness. This means that if we give it the right stimuli, it will heal itself from the impact of the adverse events.

In part 3, I will talk in more detail about how to give it the right stimuli. When we do so, your thoughts slow down and even stop. The images fade away and become difficult to see, and the emotions ease, soothing into peace. At the same time, the activations in your physical body calm down until they completely dissolve. Once this has happened, as you connect back to the adverse event, you will experience it in a completely different way. You will connect with it and be at peace. It will then seem distant and just something that happened in your past.

This indicates that the brain has now effectively integrated the memory and it is no longer encapsulated. Afterwards, you will find that you feel differently. You will feel calmer, less rigid in your thinking, and your body will feel less tense and more coordinated.

For me these are indications that the alterations in the areas of the brain, as described in the Amen Clinic study, are being healed. As we work through all the adverse events, they become healed. For many people this is enough for the nervous system to come completely into safety. It is also enough for their body to release its body's survival response, i.e., to stop doing the dystonic movements.

For other people their nervous systems get most of the way there. However, they require just a little more help. In these cases, I show the person how to teach their nervous system how to feel completely safe. I also show them how to release what's left of the automated dystonic movements from their basal ganglia and replace it with a beautiful, fluid and technically precise movement. I will show you all of this in part 3 of the book.

As I have been writing this, a trumpeter who came to me with embouchure focal dystonia springs to mind. Louise had experienced all three of the causes that we have looked at so far. She was adopted and, therefore, had experienced the most devastating attachment break that exists. She had studied her music degree at a highly pressured and oppressive music school. Whilst she was studying her degree, she had a deeply traumatic experience when she met her birth mother. It was an event that she had been unable to assimilate.

In the lead up to preparing for her recital exam, each time she played the trumpet, she felt her chin pulling upwards, she lost all strength in the muscles on the left side of her mouth, and her tongue felt hard and stuck to the roof of her mouth. She had developed focal dystonia. Shortly after finishing her degree, she had to completely give up playing the trumpet. Louise's story, like so many I hear, was heart wrenching. Music had been her life. From such a young age, all she had dreamt about was playing the trumpet. Professionally, nothing else interested her. Spiritually, it was what gave life meaning.

She contacted me nearly thirty years later. She had plucked up the courage to pick up the trumpet again, and her heart sank to find that the focal embouchure dystonia was still there, as strong as it had been when she had first abandoned her dreams.

As I worked with Louise to release the impact of the adverse events and helped her repair the attunement break of her adoption, the focal dystonia simply faded away. For me, Louise was an example of the direct relationship between these experiences and the body's expression of them in focal dystonia. She did not require me to do any work to "repair" her embouchure. Simply by enabling her brain to release these encapsulated memories and effectively integrate them, the focal dystonia resolved itself.

Chapter Seven
Injuries

Injuries are the last of the four causes of the activation in the nervous system.

I am not only referring to injuries that might have occurred whilst playing your instrument or of over practicing. I am talking about all the injuries that you might have had no matter how insignificant they might seem.

Let me give you an example. Many years ago, I worked with a basketball player who had focal dystonia in his right knee. He was famous for his speed and acceleration. He would receive the ball at the far end of the court. His acceleration was so impressive that no one from the opposite team could keep up with him. By the time he reached midcourt, he was moving so fast it was impossible for anyone to try to steal the ball without fouling him. Suddenly, his winning attribute as a player came to an end. Each time he would get close to full speed, his right knee would become rigid and lock-up completely. A colleague of his who I had helped recover from foot dystonia recommended that he contact me. At that point, his knee dystonia had caused a relatively serious knee injury, and the management of the team had told him they would not renew his contract. He felt broken, with the shards of his hard-fought sports career scattering across the floor.

Like most athletes, he had experienced several injuries whilst training and in games. Most of them were relatively minor. Unlike most of the people I work with, he had not experienced any other significant adverse events. He had grown up in a stable, attuned and supportive family. He had played for teams that had a positive culture and with warm and encouraging coaches. What came as a surprise was the principal cause of his focal knee dystonia.

In the first session, as we centred in on the dystonia, a memory from when he was seven years old spontaneously flooded in. He had been playing with his cousins and cut his head. It was really quite a minor injury. However, head injuries bleed profusely. The amount of blood and his parents', aunts' and uncles' reactions to it was highly impactful. After working through the memory of this injury, which had nothing to do with playing basketball, most of the focal dystonia disappeared. He was taken aback that this insignificant injury as a child could be the underlying cause of his focal knee dystonia. What was left of it dissipated completely as we released the memories of all the other injuries he had sustained.

So how is it that injuries can have such an impact? For the brain and nervous system, any physical injury is potentially life-threatening in several ways (remember, our brain's response assumes that we still live in the wild without modern conveniences and medicine):

- It can be the result of an aggression, an adverse event that the brain registered as a survival moment.

- It could become infected and, therefore, be life-threatening.
- It might prevent us from being able to search for food.
- It leaves us as vulnerable prey for any predator.

Therefore, the brain becomes hypervigilant, in its neuroceptive capacity, to any circumstances that are similar to how the injury took place. In chapter 1 we talked about the neuroception that is constantly occurring in the brain. Through your five senses and your limbic resonance, your brain is constantly scanning the environment for signs of safety or threat. Remember, it is doing so at about eleven million bits of perceptual information per second.

In addition, the body will often take on a protective posture to protect the injured area of the body. Sometimes, these protective postures become automated in the brain. If this is the case, many other muscles need to create compensatory tensions in response. This leads the brain and nervous system to believe that it is still under threat. It also further heightens the dissociation from the physical body (as we talked about in chapter 2), thereby reducing the interoceptive sensitivity and distorting the internal map of the body.

Any surgical operations you have had would be considered an injury. Your subcortex is unable to distinguish it from any other injury. At this level of your brain, it is unable to connect the necessity of the operation for your health with the physical impact of it. At this level, your brain and your nervous system have registered the incision and all of the physical aspects of the operation. Even though you did not feel pain due to the anaesthetic, your nervous system still registered all the physical impacts of the intervention. In addition, if it was done under general anaesthetic, it will also remember your inability to move and your complete physical defencelessness. This means that as part of your recovery from focal dystonia, it is important to explore all the injuries that you have had and release any encapsulated memories they have created.

I regularly see the relationship between injuries and focal dystonia. It is relatively frequent that an injury is the straw that breaks the camel's back. There is already an accumulation of the other causes in the nervous system, and therefore, it is already activated into survival mode. An injury then occurs, which seems to spill this activation over into the body, and the dystonic movements begin.

Part Three

Practical Steps To Dissolve Your Focal Dystonia

Chapter Eight

Tapping into Your Brain's Capacity to Heal

I hope that, in part 1 and part 2, I have helped you understand that the focal dystonia is not in your body. Therefore, it will not be resolved by working on your body.

We have seen that the cause of your focal dystonia is the hyper- or hypoactivation of your nervous system. This in turn has its primary causes. What lies underneath it are adverse events that you have experienced. They have created physical changes in your limbic system and become encapsulated in your mid and deep brain. In this way they create a constant sense of alert in your nervous system.

As we said, these experiences might have been any adverse event—in addition to the specific ones like lack of attunement, an attachment break in your childhood, having been educated in general and/or taught music within the Oppression Model, or any injuries that you may have had.

The good news is that all this can be healed. Your brain is predisposed to be healthy. This means that the right stimuli will open the gates for it to rapidly heal itself. Part 3 of this book is dedicated to showing you how to give those stimuli to your brain.

Before we move on, let's just take a moment to marvel at the miracle that is your brain. On the next clear night, take a moment to look up at the stars and particularly at the Milky Way. Perhaps if you close your eyes right now, you can see it in your mind's eye. Open your mind to its enormity. Allow yourself to have the sense of just how many stars it contains. You can see them all clustered together, seemingly into eternity. I told you to "begin to have the sense" of how many there are, because it seems to me that our conscious mind is unable to really comprehend the enormity of it. Mine certainly can't. Now let's use our imagination and senses to feel it. Multiply that sense by about four thousand. This is how many synapses, otherwise known as neural connections, that you have in your brain.

Even more, each neurone is like a star, with each point connecting to a point in another star. That one is also connected to many other neurones at each point of its star-like form. As we imagine this, we can feel how our brain is a radiant network of connections. Each star is connected to many other ones. It has a seemingly infinite complexity and beauty. It is as if we have a whole, interconnected universe inside our heads. Perhaps you can feel that sense of sublime beauty and infinite possibilities.

I would now like us to add yet another marvel. Your brain is not set in stone, as was once believed. In the past twenty years, numerous neuroscientific studies have shown the constant and remarkable capacity in the brain for neuroplasticity and neurogenesis. This means that the brain is constantly breaking connections between neurones that no longer serve it. At the same time, it is constantly creating new connections that are beneficial. If that isn't enough, it is able to constantly create completely new neurones (neurogenesis). It can do all this throughout the whole of our lives.

Let's just give some time and space to really let that sink in. Allow yourself to lean into the sense of the universe of neural connections that are in your brain. Open yourself to feeling how they are radiantly connected in a sublime infinity of possibilities. Finally, let go as you submerge yourself into thinking of how all those possibilities can be changed and improved as your brain constantly creates new neurones, reforming existing connections based on the stimuli and experiences you give it. Your subcortex is doing so at eleven million bits of perceptual information per second.

Knowing this, can you ever go back to doubting its capacity to completely heal your focal dystonia?

The only missing piece at this stage is for you to know the experiences and stimuli that it needs to do so.

Something Important to Know Before We Begin

Before we go on, there is an important key concept for you to understand. Its name is "regulation".

When your nervous system is in survival mode, i.e., when it is hyper- or hypoactivated, it is **dys**regulated.

When it is in safe mode, it is regulated.

In a little while, I will show you a technique called Brainspotting, which was created and developed by the psychologist David Grand. I had been intuitively looking for this technique professionally, throughout my whole career and personally my whole adult life. It gave me the answers I had been searching for. With laser precision it enabled me to heal the dark chasm of suffering that I carried inside me. It was a game changer for my clients as I used it to enable them to, with the same laser precision, resolve their difficulties.

Although I will not go fully into all the details of Brainspotting, I wanted to mention it here to help you understand the importance of regulating your nervous system.

A brainspot is a place where we fix our gaze, creating a specific angle in our optic nerve. In this book, we are using self-spotting. If you have worked with a Brainspotting therapist, they may well have helped you by using a pointer and been able to add some other tools. These are too complex for me to teach you in this book. However, the simple tools I am teaching you here are very powerful and all you need for activations that you can self-regulate.

Picking up the thread again, the brainspot creates an angle in your optic nerve. This angle stimulates a specific neural network. It is as if whilst we look out at the brainspot, we are really looking inwards inside our brain and nervous system.

Brainspotting enables you to connect directly to each of the neural networks that initiates the survival state in your nervous system. However, as you do so, you are actually in the safety of the here and now. As we connect to these neural networks, we are connecting to the adverse events that are encapsulated there.

When we are Brainspotting, it is like we are in two places at the same time. As we connect to the encapsulated adverse event, we experience it as having opened the capsule. In this way, the direct activation of the event or events dysregulate the nervous system, as if we are right back there in the past. At the same time, we are in this second place of awareness, safe and comfortable in the **here and now**. As we observe and feel into all the activation, our deep brain (subcortex) understands that it is a past event and no longer a threat. In this way, it regulates the nervous system and reintegrates the memory into the brain as something that happened in the past. It feels as if the brain has kept all the positive learning from what happened.

However, it does so in a calm and healthy way so the event or events can be released and left in the past where they belong.

You may be wondering what you would do if you can't really remember what happened. I will explain this later, but for now, rest assured that this will not slow you down. There are many ways of accessing the relevant, encapsulated neural networks without needing to have clear memories of past events.

Coming back to the theme of regulation and dysregulation, as I walk you through the activities and Brainspotting exercises that will enable you to cure your focal dystonia, you will find that you will easily complete many of them. When the activation that occurs is relatively low, you can self-regulate it. This means that on your own, you can keep enough of yourself anchored into the here and now, and your brain can bring the activation of the nervous system down and back into safe mode.

However, there will be Brainspotting exercises and other activities where this is not the case. In those, you will find that the activation is too strong and pulls you fully back into the past, or you will disconnect and be unable to effectively focus on them. In these exercises, it is necessary for you to work with a Brainspotting therapist who has been trained by me in my Focal Dystonia Cure Method. As you are supported through these exercises by an expert, they become your anchor and ensure that enough of your brain stays in the here and now. As I just explained, this is necessary for it to calm your nervous system into safety and create the changes in your neural connections. When this happens, these memories become healthily reintegrated in your brain.

This phenomenon is called coregulation and has a clear scientific explanation. In the middle of your brain lies what is sometimes called your mammal brain. Its technical name is the limbic system. In fact, we talked earlier about this part of the brain and how the Amen Clinic study showed that alterations occur in it whilst experiencing adverse events. I explained the relationship between these changes and focal dystonia.

Our limbic system is the part of the brain that is involved in our emotional and behavioural responses. It is one of the most complex parts of the brain and is responsible for much of our social behaviour, connection and communication, particularly nonverbal communication.

In chapter 4 we talked about how attunement is vital for human babies and children. I mentioned limbic resonance, which is the capacity for empathy and connection where people become attuned to each other's inner states.

When you are accompanied by a therapist in your Brainspotting you create limbic resonance with them and them with you. This means that they are sensing your activation in their limbic system. At the same time, they stay in a state of deep calm and safety in their nervous system. Your limbic system is simultaneously connected to and resonates with their calmness. This acts as the anchor that holds you in the here and now and into well-being. It enables your brain to process your activation until it comes into complete calmness. Your therapist will follow how you are feeling and, if necessary, will connect to you verbally, acting as an even stronger anchor.

It is especially important to work with a skilled therapist if one of the underlying causes of your focal dystonia is having received lack of attunement as a child or having experienced an attachment break. By definition, it is necessary for you to be held in an attuned relationship as you heal the activation caused in your nervous system. Your brain needs to touch on the sense of survival, disconnection, loneliness and not being enough whilst it is in a therapeutic relationship where you feel safe, connected, held and accepted just the way you are. Only through this holding can it know what attunement feels like.

Therefore, through the midst of your pain, connected to these young parts of your brain, you can relive your lonely experiences. However, this time, you will be well accompanied in a highly attuned relationship. As this happens, your brain begins to feel as if it had always been held in this attunement, and fear and survival fade into peace and safety.

I would just like to make a very relevant aside at this point. If your story includes a lack of attunement or attachment breaks in your childhood, it is very possible that you became highly self-sufficient. If this is the case, you have probably resolved most of the challenges that life has put before you on your own, with your own capacities and inner resources. This self-sufficiency probably feels very familiar and safe, albeit a lonely and exhausting place to function from. It may well feel safe because you know that you can depend on yourself. This means that it is accompanied by a sense of feeling that others cannot be depended on, and eventually, they will be a source of pain for you and will let you down. You may well be convinced of the truth of this.

However, this very sense is one of the key activations in your nervous system. It is one of the key underlying causes of your focal dystonia. The truth is that our nervous system is wired to need connection to others for our well-being. It needs the level of connection that we only find through attuned limbic resonance to feel safe. It needs this throughout the whole of our life.

It is true that as small children we need much more constant attunement. This is because our brain has not yet developed the capacity to self-regulate and we are dependent on the coregulation that the attuned adults around us provide. Through their attunement our emotions calm down. As we get older, our brain develops an ever-increasing capacity to soothe ourselves and self-regulate emotions. As adults, we do have the capacity to functionally self-regulate very effectively. However, it has been clearly demonstrated that we also have an inbuilt need to have attuned and coregulatory experiences. Without them our nervous system develops background activation.

If you recognise this self-sufficiency in yourself, you may well feel that you want to cure your focal dystonia on your own. You may feel that you want to shut yourself away and quietly work through the exercises on your own until you have resolved your focal dystonia. However, you are completely absorbed into one of the mental expressions of your focal dystonia. You are being as dystonic as your body is when the muscles become rigid, contracted, weak, trembling or spasmodic.

The only way for you to heal is by allowing yourself to be accompanied by a well-trained expert. In that way their calm attunement to you will enable this activation in your nervous system to come into well-being. Often the most difficult aspects for us to heal are the activations that feel so familiar that we believe them to be normal and even healthy. These are exactly the activations that we need an expert professional perspective to support us in healing.

If you experienced a lack of attunement in your childhood, you may experience a couple of other feelings of resistance to asking for professional help. I would like to mention them here so that you understand how they are expressions of the activation in your nervous system. Moreover, I want you to understand that the attunement you will receive from an expert therapist is essential for you to heal. I hope that through this comprehension, you will overcome your resistance and will reach out and ask for help.

When we are babies and very small children, our parents are the complete authority on everything. Therefore, if our faith in them was broken through an attachment break, lack of attunement, or from them being actively mis-attuned as is the case in physical, emotional or mental abuse, we might have transferred that break to everything that represents authority. This means that we may feel much resistance because of our fear of putting ourselves in the hands of an expert. We may feel that in a therapeutic relationship, we are in a vulnerable position and can't trust the therapist to have that much authority over us.

I would like you to rest assured that Brainspotting therapy differs significantly from many other therapies. It does so in several ways:

- You are in control of the session. You will choose the theme that you would like to work on and maintain control of the process throughout. The therapist uses their expertise to give you relevant information so you can choose the best way to work for you. After all, you are the expert on you. You are the only person who knows what is going on inside you.
- The central focus of your Brainspotting therapist is their attunement to you. This means they are focused on what you are telling them. It also means they will follow what you need. They understand that if they were to impose their ideas on you or be directive, they would be acting out of the Oppression Model with you. Brainspotting is fundamentally rooted in the Liberation Model. I imagine that by now you are getting a sense of what the Liberation Model feels like.

The other related area of resistance that you might have is feeling that the therapist is not good enough for you. In a way, this resistance has the same source. If we have felt so hurt, let down and lonely, we might feel that only a perfect therapist will be safe enough for us to work with. However, an innate problem with this feeling is that no one on the face of the earth is perfect, and we can always find a flaw in everyone. The reality is that it is important to ensure we work with someone who has the necessary skills and capacities to support us in our process. The reality is, also, that this is enough and we don't need anything more. The therapists that you can contact through my website are trained personally with me and have regular supervision sessions with me. I directly oversee that they are skilled and capable in working with you.

As I describe this, I remember Esteban who attended one of my masterclasses. It was a situation that left me feeling sad, as I was unable to reach him.

Whilst he listened to the information I shared, he only wanted to engage with it from his neocortex. He found our first two exercises, which are the foundation of everything, difficult to do. However, he was not open to receiving any support in his process. He told me that he could heal himself and that he wanted to do so on his own. It was difficult for him to see his blind spots, and at that point, reaching out for help felt too challenging for him.

I did my best to create an attuned and trusting relationship with him. However, it was not enough to reach him.

A year later, as I write this, the other people who attended the class are all dystonia free. Unfortunately, I see from his social media posts that he is still struggling with his focal dystonia.

I want you to know that there is a great amount of progress you can make on your own. You can heal all the activations that you can self-regulate; however, there will be activations that are too intense or that originate in an attachment break or a mis-attunement that you experienced as a child. On your own, your nervous system will be unable to heal them. Therefore, even though you might feel resistance in reaching out to a therapist, it is necessary to do so. Your nervous system will only heal and come into safety through the attuned presence of a therapist who is an expert in this field.

Chapter Nine

Ready to Go to the Next Stage

I f you have been doing the Attunement Repair Exercise regularly, you are already well on your way with stage 1 of your recovery.

In preparation to go on to the next stage, I would like to walk you through a review of how stage 1 is coming along. This review is fundamentally important. I have been peppering the focal dystonia mentality throughout the book. These are the mental patterns created because of the changes that occur in your limbic system from the adverse events you have experienced.

One of those mental aspects is a feeling of needing to get to the end as soon as possible. Sometimes this comes from feeling uncomfortable with the uncertainty that is a natural part of any change process. Whilst we are taking the steps, we do not know 100 percent if we are going to achieve the results we want. This uncertainty feels uncomfortable, and so we are tempted to rush through the steps to escape it and reach the certain ground of having achieved the result we want.

The other common reason stems from the underlying mentality of not feeling good enough. From this feeling, some people can fall into the trap of wanting to prove they are special or gifted and, therefore, will cure themselves quicker than anyone else.

Whatever underlying motivation is occurring, if you try to hurry through the exercises, this will work against you. It will have two consequences:

First, you will go slower and find it more difficult. This is because each exercise builds on the previous one. By consolidating an exercise before moving on, the next one will be an easy next step, which you will become good at much quicker than if you move on too soon.

Second, you will create gaps in your healing, which might result in your becoming stuck further along the path and not reaching a full resolution of your focal dystonia. Later on, it is difficult to identify where these gaps are to fill them.

This means that to heal your focal dystonia in the smoothest and swiftest way, you want to be kindly meticulous with each exercise before moving to the next one. Sink into the process to be fully present with and enjoy each moment of it, without thinking or analysing where it is taking you. If you get stuck on any given exercise, or if it is difficult for you, this is a sign that you would benefit from professional help. In this case I encourage you to contact a Brainspotting therapist, via my website, who is trained in my Focal Dystonia Cure Method.

The exercises are designed to take you in comfortable incremental steps towards a complete resolution of your focal dystonia. They are also designed to connect with the activation in your nervous system. This means that in themselves they are simple exercises, but this does not mean you will find them easy. As they touch on your activation, if it is the type that requires coregulation to heal, by definition the exercise will be very difficult for you. It may even feel impossible. Be kind to yourself and reach out for support.

I would like us to take a little aside into kindness. Another of the dystonia mental patterns is the demanding and criticism and we often direct towards ourselves. If you find yourself pushing, criticising or feeling frustrated with yourself in the journey we are taking, then in that moment your nervous system is activated. In that moment you are in the middle of one of the causes of your focal dystonia. The antidote is kindness.

When you are connected to the part of your limbic system that creates the feelings of kindness, you are at the same time connecting to the part of your brain that self-regulates your nervous system. This means that as you strengthen these feelings of kindness, at the same time, you strengthen your ability to move your nervous system out of survival and into safety. This in turn will allow your body to release the dystonic movements that the survival mode is creating. The third stage on this journey is focused on how to develop and deepen into kindness.

For now, let's come back to see how you are getting on with the Attunement Repair Exercise I gave you in chapter 3 and how to know when you are ready to move to stage 2.

Some questions are listed below to help you get a gauge of where you are and where to take it from here. If you have not been able to do the exercise because it has been too activating for you, or because you have not been able to connect at all with it, this indicates that you require coregulatory support from an expert therapist. If you have been able to do the exercise, ensure that you have done it at least twenty times over three to five weeks before answering the questions.

I have written a series of statements. Tick the ones that are true to you:

1. When I do the exercise, I scan my body and see where it is tense and where it is relaxed.
2. When I do the exercise, I feel like I am inhabiting my body and can feel all or nearly all of it from the inside.
3. I can feel some areas of my body, but there are also significant areas that seem blank or that I just can't connect with.
4. I find the exercise rather boring.
5. I am becoming more and more aware of the infinite number of sensations that are occurring inside of me, all the time.
6. I notice myself being more inside my body and less in my head, in general, throughout the day.
7. I haven't noticed any real difference throughout the day.

If you feel like statements 2, 5 and 6 are true to you, you are ready to move onto stage 2.

If you relate more to statements 1, 3, 4 and 7, I encourage you to continue with the exercise. If you continue to feel this way, it indicates an activation in your nervous system that requires coregulation for it to become released. In which case, I suggest that your next step is to be kind to yourself and to reach out for some expert support.

I hope that you have been kindly honest with yourself as you answered the questions. As I mentioned before, you will not be doing yourself any favours by moving on to stage 2 until the Attunement Repair Exercise is truly consolidated.

If you do honestly feel ready to move on, I suggest that you continue to do the Attunement Repair Exercise regularly throughout the whole of this journey. The exercise has many benefits for you. The two most important ones are the following:

You will become increasingly connected to and aware of yourself, which will enable you to see better the pernicious activations you are not aware of yet. They are the ones that feel so familiar and have become so normalised that you don't recognise them as activations.

Part of the foundation of our journey is the development of your interoceptive sensitivity. This is a skill that requires time and patience to develop and even more so for those of us who have experienced adverse events. You will be very grateful towards yourself, at the end of the process when we connect with any residual dystonic movements, if you take the time to fine-tune this skill. That is exactly what is happening as you practice this exercise. The greater your interoceptive sensitivity at the end of our journey, the easier it will be to release what is left of the dystonic movements.

Finally, before we move on, I wanted to remind you to let go of pushing and trying. It is tempting with these exercises to try hard to get them right or to push yourself to feel more. However, if you do so, you will be inhibiting the part of the brain that can easily complete the exercises. I know that it can be difficult to let go of this habit, as many of us have been taught from a young age that it is the only way to get things done and be successful. However, it is like trying to remember a name. The more you try, the more it escapes you.

In these exercises, you want to take a different approach and thereby connect with a different part of your brain. You will do so by opening yourself up and allowing yourself to deepen or fall into the experience. In this way, all that is necessary is to just be present with what is, in complete acceptance and trust. What you are experiencing, however little or much, is just perfect for you in that moment. As you are consistent in practicing, your skills will develop at exactly the right pace for you.

Chapter Ten
Stage 2 - Coming into Balance

I think that you are keen to keep moving forward. Therefore, without further ado, I would like to walk you through the following exercise, which is the foundation for stage 2 of your journey. Afterwards, I will explain the context of this stage. This exercise is called the Zero-State Exercise. I give it that name because it brings your thoughts, emotions and body into balance.

In all the remaining exercises that I give you in the book, you might listen through headphones to David Grand's bilateral sounds. These are tracks he has specially recorded, where the sound passes from one ear to the other. As they do so, they help to bring the nervous system into calmness and support the balance between the left and right side of the brain. David has released numerous bilateral CDs. If you are a musician, I suggest that you listen to the tracks that are just nature sounds, rather than the music tracks. I find that many musicians find the musical tracks distracting in a way that the nature sounds are not.

. . .

92

Exercise:

Zero-State Exercise

Find a place that is quiet and comfortable and where you won't be disturbed for about ten to fifteen minutes.

I recommend that you do this exercise sitting down or standing up. Explore both and find what feels best to you.

Once you are ready, listen to the bilateral sounds through your headphones and follow these steps:

1. Close your eyes and, from your memory, at your own pace, do the Attunement Repair Exercise until you reach the area of your hips. Once you are there, you will be feeling the inner sensations of your feet, lower legs, knees, thighs, glutes and the whole of your hip area at the same time.

2. Bring the centre of your attention to your hip bones. You can feel that they form a bowl shape. Take a moment to really feel them.

3. Begin to feel inwards into this bowl, gradually moving towards the centre of it. Take the time you need. You may find that you can bring your attention right to the centre the first time you do this exercise. It is as equally likely that you will need to do it several times over the next few days until your attention can feel this deeply. There is really no hurry. Give yourself the time you need and kindly accept your experience just the way it is. Have you heard the saying "more haste, less speed"? This is especially relevant for these exercises. The more you try to hurry or feel you should be able to do it better as soon as possible, the

slower you will go. If you open yourself to feeling inwards, you will eventually feel right into the centre.

4. Once you can feel into the centre of the bowl that your hips make, bring all of your attention there and feel into it for three to five minutes.

It is important for you to consolidate this step before moving on. Therefore, I recommend that you repeat steps 1 to 4 for at least four more days before moving on to step 5. If you feel like you would like to do so for even longer, follow your inner sense of what you need and only move on when you feel ready.

It is especially important to consolidate this step before moving on. Much of the rest of the journey depends on this step feeling solid. If it is not, everything else will be built on a shaky foundation. The further down the path we go, the more you will notice this lack of solidity. Let's invest in yourself at this point and give yourself all the time you need until you really feel this consolidation.

As you feel into the centre of the bowl that your hips form, notice how it changes your inner state. Notice how your thoughts become more still and how your mind becomes clearer. Notice how you feel more stable, peaceful and calm. Many people report that they feel more confident and balanced. As you continue to feel into it, become increasingly present to and aware of the state that it automatically creates in you.

5. In step 4 you were feeling into the physical centre of gravity of your body. This creates a bottom-to-top balance in your brain and nervous system. Now we want to add to it the side-to-side balance. To do so, you need to keep feeling into the centre of gravity and, at the same time, become aware that there is a space running up and down the centre of your body. This is the space that is neither the left nor the right side, nor front or back of you. It is the space in between them that joins them together.

As you keep feeling into your centre of gravity, bring both sides of your mind inwards and into this central space until your mind has fully dropped into it. Do so without losing your presence and feeling of the centre of gravity.

As you practice this over the following days, it will become more and more easy. Keep practicing it until it feels strongly consolidated. Then you will be ready to move to step 6.

6. By now you will feel deeply connected to and present with both the centre of gravity and the central vertical space at the same time. As you feel into and maintain your inward connection to both, slowly—almost incidentally—open your eyes. If you keep your attention feeling inwards, you will find that your eyes will be automatically fixed on a particular place to maintain this connection. Let them rest there for another three to five minutes as you feel into your centre of gravity, central vertical space, and the mental, emotional and physical state that it creates. It is almost

as if your eyes aren't looking outwards at all, but rather that they are looking inwards.

7. When you are ready to finish, slowly listen to the sounds that are surrounding you and allow your eyes to become aware of the room around you. Use all your senses to connect once again to the outer world. You will find a point of balance where you feel your connection to your zero-state, and at the same time, you are fully back to the here and now. You are ready to continue with your day.

You have now taken all the steps to fully develop the zero-state. You have also had your first experience of Brainspotting, if you haven't had so before. From here, you will need to practice this exercise regularly, preferably every day. You will find that as you do, you will connect with the centre of gravity and then the central vertical space almost instantly. Once this is possible, the exercise will only take you about five minutes to complete. Do so with your eyes open and looking at the brainspot that helps you connect to the state.

As you do this, use the exercise to feel increasingly deeper into your centre of gravity and your central vertical space. You will find that the deeper you drop into them, the more silence you will find there. Allow yourself to be absorbed into this silence and to feel and listen to it with all your attention. It is as if you can let go and drop deeper into the silence. Over the days and weeks, you will find that your interoceptive sensitivity of this silence increases. As it does so, it becomes an ever more tangible part of who you are. You will find that you can profoundly connect with it with ease as it becomes a material sense of being for you. As it does so, you will become aware of how many constructed identities you have created through your search for feeling you are "enough", such as needing to be the best or better, to be recognised by others or even to be the suffering artist. You will feel how superficial and exhausting they are, and above all how much they make you suffer. You may experience how they drive you to be constantly in your head and in the past or the future. As you deepen into the physical feelings of the centre of gravity in your body, in the pelvic bowl area, you drop into the embodiment of this silence. It is that easy. There is no need to try or make an effort. You simply let go into a sense of your essence where you are just simply in profound stillness and well-being. It is a feeling that your thinking brain is unable to grasp nor understand. However, as you let go of the need to comprehend it, you have a direct experience of it and simply feel that you are "enough". You feel the futility of all your normal mental activity and how it is centred around trying to manipulate the world to be the way you want it to be. Here, as the spaciousness of the here and now opens up and embraces you, everything drops into place, and you let go of fighting against the reality of what is.

George approached me to help him with his writer's cramp. He captured my attention with his capacity to connect with this silence. It was beautiful to witness how deeply he dropped into this sublime and wise place within himself. He described it as pure bliss and profound wordless intelligence. He told me that it created a deep connection to his essence and sense of self. He found himself free of self-doubt and criticism. He was especially delighted with how his creativity became liberated. He began to experience an ease and flow of ideas that he never had before. He told me that the quality of his writing had taken a quantum leap.

Whilst George's experience stood out for being so deep and sublime, it reflects a key moment that we all reach on this journey. It is the release of one of the key dystonic mental patterns, which is reflected in our misplaced identity. One of the most significant mental patterns is feeling identified with as an external measure of your worth. For musicians, this is often on their virtuosity, or the recognition that they receive. They feel and believe that this is who they are. As you become adept with and deeply connected to the silence inside your zero-state, you connect with a deeper and more authentic sense of who you are. If you can allow yourself to let go and fall into this silent space, you will be amazed at the peace, strength, wisdom and genius you will find there.

I will go into more details about Brainspotting in a short while. However, I thought you might like to know why I have guided you to open your eyes once you are deeply connected to the state, letting your eyes automatically go where they will help you maintain this connection. This is called the brainspot for the state. You will probably find that they will go to the same place each time. If at some point, the brainspot changes, this is also fine. Trust that your brain knows what it is doing.

As your eyes fix on this brainspot, your optic nerve is influencing your brain, stimulating the neural networks that create this state in you. As it does, it enhances your ability to connect with and deepen into it. We are stimulating the learning capacity of the brain.

You can think of the neural networks like pathways. Here is a metaphor for them. If you were to go to the countryside and walk through some untrodden grass, you would leave a mark in it. However, if you went back to that same place a week later, you wouldn't see where you had walked the previous week. Yet if, on the other hand, you had walked the same path every day over that week, you would have left quite a mark. Over time, it would become indelible, so even if you went away for a while, when you came back, the path would still be there.

You can begin to see that the more frequently you use a path, the more permanent it becomes. There is another factor to be aware of, and that is the more traffic that goes down that path, the wider it becomes. Just think about a motorway, as we call it in the UK. It can sustain a huge amount of high-velocity traffic.

If we apply this back to our brain, we want to make these healthy and helpful neural networks like motorways. The technical term for this is *myelination*. At the same time, we want the dystonic networks to become like disused roads. As we have just seen, we strengthen the neural networks by frequency of use and by having a high amount of traffic running through them. This is why I encourage you to practice the exercise every day.

We increase the amount of traffic in two principal ways:

Through a high level of interoceptive sensitivity, the better you can feel and connect to all the subtle sensations and experiences that occur on the inside whilst you do the exercise, the greater the traffic down the neural network.

You will also increase traffic by applying the state in as many different situations as possible. We are not yet at this stage, but you will get there, and I will walk you through step-by-step how to do so.

At this point, to strengthen the neural network and increase your skill with the zero-state, all you need to focus on is:

- Doing the exercise frequently, preferably every day.
- Doing it with as much presence and interceptive sensitivity as you can. If you have completed the Attunement Repair Exercise meticulously, you will now begin to reap the rewards of it.

As you do it with your eyes looking at the brainspot, you accelerate the process of myelination. You also strengthen the access that you have to this state. You will find that over time, it becomes easier to connect with it, and you do so at an increasingly deep level.

If the brainspot changes at any time, I believe this indicates the neuroplasticity of your brain and how the state is developing with it. It would make sense that as your brain develops, strengthens and deepens this state, it may connect to more neural networks and change to improve the connections it had initially. This could well lead to a new brainspot, which will take you to this expanded and deeper experience of the state.

As with all the exercises in this book, if you have found that the Zero-State Exercise is uncomfortable and activating for you, or if you find it difficult to do or connect with, reach out for expert help. With this help, you will be able to do this exercise. You can imagine the number of people I have helped over my more than thirty years of experience. Every single person, with the right support, has been successful entering into and deepening their zero-state.

Chapter 11

Stage 3 - Coming Home to Safety

Let's take a moment to rise to the helicopter view of the journey I am guiding you through. It is very useful to take this overview every now and again. It helps you remember where you started and where you are going.

We began with establishing that your focal dystonia is not in your body. It is your body's response to the experiences that you have had, which have put your nervous system into survival mode. These experiences may be any combination of lack of attunement or an attachment break when you were a child, having been raised or taught within the Oppression Model, an injury, or any other adverse event.

This means that your focal dystonia is not a problem to be gotten rid of. Rather, it is a welcome guest that is communicating to you with deep wisdom.

You may be very aware of some of the aspects of the survival mode in your nervous system. They may be symptoms such as anxiety, panic attacks, phobias, being hijacked by anger or rage, or depression. However, many other aspects, especially the more subtle ones, may be so familiar to you that you think they are normal or beneficial. These include demanding of yourself to be better than you are, the desire to be admired and recognised by others, self-criticism, feeling competitive towards others, comparing yourself to them, feeling superior or inferior, making rigid plans for your practice and expected progress, the impostor syndrome, feeling chaotic or disorganised, feeling separated or isolated from others, wanting to keep yourself separate or distant from others, being in your head and your thoughts, being unaware of your body most of the time, having moments where you feel confused or where your mind goes blank, having moments or situations you feel that you can't face, feeling like there just isn't enough time, and doubting yourself in certain situations. I could go on, and I am sure that you can relate to many of these descriptions.

Therefore, we began our journey at a practical level with the Attunement Repair Exercise. This exercise helps you to reconnect to yourself and your physical body. This is important because the survival mode in your nervous system causes disconnection, technically called dissociation, from your physical body and sense of self. As you become practiced and skilled at the exercise, you are at the same time increasing your interoceptive sensitivity. This is your ability to feel yourself from the inside to highly subtle levels. You will develop this sensitivity to your inner physical, mental and emotional worlds. As you do so, you will become more aware of and more able to recognise the subtle expressions of the survival mode in your nervous system.

This awareness, from a place within yourself of acceptance and respect, is the first and most important step in your transformation. It is also a key aspect of stepping into the Liberation Model.

I am not saying that the survival mode is wrong. It is completely understandable. Moreover, given the experiences that you have had, it was completely natural and wise for your nervous system to become stuck in survival. Therefore, at no time do we want to push or cajole it into changing. If we did, we would be simply compounding the experiences that it has had and give it even more reasons to grip on tightly to the protection it gave you.

We are taking a completely different approach. We are listening and feeling deeply into what is occurring on the inside of you. We are doing so from a place of honouring and respecting the experiences you have had and the wisdom of your nervous system and body in its response to them. Above all, we are honouring and respecting how these responses have protected you and kept you safe. Through the exercises we will complete on this journey, we would simply like to, from the deepest respect, give it other choices about how to keep you safe, but with your nervous system being profoundly seated in its safe mode.

With the Zero-State Exercise, we have now begun to enter, comprehend and strengthen the safe mode in your nervous system.

The next exercise gives another paradigm to this safe mode. As it does so, it literally develops and strengthens the areas of your brain that resolve the activations in your nervous system. In addition, it heals the alterations in your brain that were created by the adverse events you experienced.

The fourth stage of our journey, which runs in parallel with your development of these initial stages, involves the deactivation of the survival state that has become stuck in your nervous system.

It runs in parallel with stage 1 and 2 because there is a positive feedback loop that becomes created between them. As you develop your connection to and strengthen safety in your nervous system, you become increasingly clear about what the activation of the survival mode feels like. This clarity will reach more subtle levels of your inner experience.

The positive feedback loop is that the more you deactivate and resolve the activation in your nervous system, the easier it is for you to drop into safety in your nervous system and into how sublime it feels. As you begin to experience the beauty and bliss of this safety, it gives new meaning to your life. You begin to comprehend your survival patterns and how futile they are. You literally enter a whole new paradigm in your being, where everything that you have experienced until now makes sense in a different way. Here you understand who you are and connect with your unique expression as an artist. Here your genius is set free from the bottle with all the security and permission it needs to just authentically be!

The journey home is often inspiring and deeply touching, as in the example of Francisco. He was particularly meticulous with developing his interoceptive sensitivity. He certainly reaped the rewards of doing so.

As he practiced the Attunement Repair and Zero-State Exercises, he became aware of how rigid the left side of his body was, yet the right side felt fluid and free. He followed my instructions to just feel into the sensations without judgement or analysis. He said that the rigidity was all about getting it right, being responsible and striving to do the best he could.

At first, he couldn't understand why this created rigidity when he deemed them to be his key values. This confusion was compounded by his sense of the fluid right side of his body feeling irresponsible and chaotic.

He allowed himself to deepen into this experience. He welcomed it even though it made no sense to him. As he interoceptively listened to it, its wisdom began to emerge. As it did, he began to perceive everything differently. He described the rigid responsibility as himself as a boy, shrinking into himself to avoid the harshness and criticism of his father. He began to realise how his discipline and desire to do everything well came from the insecurity that these experiences had engraved in him.

Through the work we did together, he connected to the freedom of the right side of his body from his inner knowing of what safety feels like. As he did this, he realised that it had only felt like chaos because of his fear of making a mistake that it subconsciously provoked in him. With this realisation, it no longer felt chaotic nor irresponsible. Instead, it felt like a part of him that was joyful and free.

Over time, he came back to wholeness. The frightened child within him realised that it could enjoy being responsible and not need to do so out of fear. He liked how this sense of inner safety felt. He was delighted with how the rigidity in the left side of his body faded away and how fluid and responsive his left hand became.

Kindness Is the Key

Over recent years, there have been many important studies on the positive effect of kindness meditations and neuro-plasticity.

The 2008, a study by the University of Wisconsin-Madison, published on March 25 in the *Public Library of Science One*, using fMRI scans, demonstrated significant changes in the brain in people who had meditated for at least ten thousand hours on loving kindness. This study showed dramatic positive changes in the limbic system, just in the areas that are damaged by adverse events. These are key areas that enable you to be attuned to yourself and others, in regulating the nervous system, in creating homeostasis, in motor control, and in increasing interoceptive sensitivity (the insula region of the brain and the temporoparietal junction).

The 2013 study by Kok et al., published in the *Psychological Science Journal* on July 1, showed the connection between meditation on loving kindness and increased self-regulation and emotional well-being through the polyvagal system. This is the system that has been shown to govern whether our nervous system is in safe or survival mode.

A study by Kearney et al., published in the *Journal of Traumatic Stress* August 26, 2013, showed how a twelve-week programme of loving kindness significantly reduced the effects of adverse events in the participants.

In 2011, Hoffmann, Grossman and Hinton (*Clinical Psychology Review*, November 2011) and in 2015, Hutcherson, Seppala and Gross (*Cognitive, Affective and Behavioural Neuroscience*, March 15, 2015) demonstrated that meditating on loving kindness increased grey matter in the areas of the brain related to emotional regulation.

I could continue, but I think that these are enough studies to demonstrate that the development of kindness is central to repair the alterations in the brain that your adverse experiences have created and to enable you to regulate your nervous system and bring it out of survival and into safety.

I am fully supportive of your exploring loving kindness meditation groups and teachers in the area where you live. At the same time, I am going to give you an exercise using Brainspotting, which will efficiently and swiftly develop and strengthen the areas in your brain that are cited in the above studies. This means that the following exercise will rapidly and effectively create the same neuroplastic and neurogenesis effect that these studies describe. This exercise is central to the journey we are taking to completely resolve the symptoms of focal dystonia you are experiencing.

. . .

Exercise:

Kindness-State Exercise

You can move on to this exercise even if you haven't mastered the Zero-State Exercise. If you have time, you can do both of them each day. If your time is more limited, alternate them, doing one of them today, the other one tomorrow, then going back to the first one the next day and so on. If you are working with a specialist therapist to heal the activation that makes the Zero-State Exercise difficult for you, you will most likely be able to begin this exercise before starting the Zero-State Exercise. Talk it through with your therapist. On many occasions, the Kindness-State Exercise helps you heal and more readily begin the Zero-State Exercise.

You will need around fifteen minutes, where you can sit in a comfortable and peaceful place, knowing you won't be disturbed. Sit comfortably, and if you wish to, turn on the bilateral sounds.

1. Close your eyes and spend some time to attune into and inhabit your physical body. You will likely find this to have become relatively easy because of your practice with the Attunement Repair Exercise. As you do this, be aware of your experience just the way it is. Welcome and feel into whatever you find, all that is comfortable and well, and at the same time, all that is uncomfortable and lacking wellness. All is welcome here; every part has something important to communicate to you and deserves your respect and care.

2. When you feel ready to move on and if you have become sufficiently adept at the Zero-State Exercise,

drop into your centre of gravity and then bring your mind into the central vertical space. Sit with this experience, attuning deeply into it. Do so for the time that feels right for you. Do take your time as you let go of that compulsive feeling of wanting to rush to the next step. Allow yourself the luxury of feeling that you have all the time and space in the world. If you are not yet skilled enough with the Zero-State Exercise, skip this step and go straight to the next one.

3. When you feel ready, connect to a situation or memory that invoked the feeling of kindness in you. Perhaps it was a time you helped a friend in need, or when you spent time with a small child. Perhaps you had rescued an injured or frightened animal, or maybe it was when you took care of someone who was ill or who was going through a difficult and painful experience. We often feel at our kindest when we can support or help someone who is very vulnerable. Choose a moment of kindness, seeing what you saw, hearing what you heard, and feeling the kindness within you.

4. Attune deeply into what that kindness felt like on the inside. How did it physically feel in your body and where did you notice it most? Take plenty of time to feel into this. Use all your interoceptive sensitivity to feel as deeply as you can into all the subtle details of this experience. You may find that it has a certain texture or colour, or you may find that it has a different sense of inner speed and space than you normally feel.

5. When you are ready, maintain this depth of connection to the physical experience of kindness, and at the

same time, become aware, also, of how it feels emotionally and mentally.

6. When you feel as deeply connected as possible to
this physical, mental and emotional experience of kindness, slowly open your eyes. As you continue to feel
deeply into it, you will find that they are looking in a
particular place to enable you to maintain this connection. Keep your eyes looking at this spot, as you
continue to feel deeply into your direct experience of
kindness. Stay here all the time you wish, really
savouring the details of this experience and letting
them spread through your whole body.

7. When you feel ready to close, gradually become
aware of the sounds that are around you, allow your
eyes to become more aware of the room surrounding
you, and use all your senses to connect back to the
outer world until you find yourself in the balance of
continuing to feel your inner kindness. At the same
time, be fully back into the here and now in the
external world that surrounds you. Now you are ready
to continue with your day.

Most people feel this sense of kindness in their chest as
warmth and softness. They feel how their heart opens and
expands. They experience their mind becoming soft and sweet.

As you practice this exercise over the days and weeks, you
will find that the experience deepens and expands into your
body until it feels like every cell and molecule of your being
becomes filled with kindness. In the same way as with the Zero-
State Exercise, you will experience the kindness-state as a state
of being. It will form into a part of your central identity from

where the world no longer feels hostile. You may realise how much beauty, warmth and holding you are surrounded by and how you had been filtering them out and had been blind to experiencing them. In this state of being, you feel safe and held in life, and you find the joy of a deep connection to the people, nature and the world around you.

It is important that you spend time and savour the Zero-State and Kindness-State Exercises. It is essential to develop your interoceptive sensitivity of the states and skills to develop and consolidate them. Through your conscious interoceptive sensitivity, your brain can accelerate the myelination of these neural networks. Using the brainspot accelerates it even more. This results in these skills and states becoming increasingly accessible, and most importantly, they become automated into your default states.

This includes the emotional and mental aspects of the state. It also, perhaps more importantly, includes the physical aspect of the states. As you will have noticed, when you enter them, the tensions in your physical body release almost instantly. Perhaps the most impactful experience I have seen of this was with Philippa. She came to me with mouse-focused writer's cramp. In other words, she had developed focal dystonia in the index finger of her right hand, in relationship to using the mouse of her computer. By the time she came to me, it had become so severe that her index finger was in constant spasms, all day and night. She described it like a constant electrical pulse running up her arm from her index finger.

In one of our early sessions, I guided her through the Kindness-State Exercise. She connected with it very easily and focused her eyes on the brainspot for this state. Almost instantly, the electrical pulse calmed right down, as did the spasms in her finger. It did not go away completely, and we are still in the early days of her process. However, the calming impact on her body and the dramatic reductions in the spasms demonstrate the powerful impact that these safe states have on our body. By just centring herself into the kindness-state, her finger went from being in constant spasms to having just one or two small twitches per minute.

Chapter 12
Deepening into Safety

As I already mentioned, stages 2 and 3 are designed to help you strengthen the sense of safety in your nervous system. Then in stage 4, I will show you how to deactivate the survival state it currently holds.

Let's stay, for now, with the theme of safety. We will develop it in two very clear phases:

1. Introverted safety
2. Extroverted safety.

I have chosen these words very specifically for their linguistic meaning. This means that they do not have any connection to the way they are used in other psychological theories. I am using them in the literal sense that *intro* means *inwards* and *extra* means *outwards*. *Ver* means *to see*. Therefore, intro-ver-ted means to see inwards, and extro-ver-ted means to see outwards.

This means that our first phase is to let go of the stimuli of the outer world and enable you to develop the state of safety in your nervous system as you look and connect inwards with yourself.

You have experienced how easy it is to shut out the external world and feel inwards on what is happening inside of you with the three exercises that I have already given you.

It is important for us to develop our introverted safe state first. This is because of all the potential activating stimuli that our nervous system is receiving from the outer world. Do you remember how we talked about the neuroception that your deep brain is constantly involved in? How your deep brain is scanning your environment at about eleven million bits of information per second? It is doing so through your five senses and your limbic resonance. It is doing so to spot signs of safety and danger.

For those of us who have experienced adverse events, a lack of infant attunement, and/or have experienced the Oppression Model, neuroception is very relevant. Anything that might be reminiscent of these experiences will be registered as danger. This could be anything, such as a colour, someone's body language or facial expression, a sound, a texture and so on. For just about all of the musicians that I have worked with, if not all of them, the sight and feel of their instrument sparks a danger response in their nervous systems.

If our nervous system is being constantly activated by stimuli from the outer world, we are asking too much of ourselves to begin to develop an extroverted safe state as our first step. First of all, we want to reduce these stimuli to a minimum whilst we begin to develop our experience of safety in the nervous system.

This is exactly what we have been doing until now, in stages 1, 2 and 3 of this journey.

At this point, we are looking for you to have been meticulously completing these exercises and to have called on expert help from a therapist, trained by me in this method, when necessary. As you do so, you will reach a point where you experience the introverted safe state in your nervous system. Take a moment to reflect on how it feels to you. I encourage you to write down your experiences.

This is how I often hear people that I work with describe how it feels and it fits like a glove with my personal experience of it:

"I feel a sense of inner peace and stability. It is as if everything slows down on the inside. My mind becomes clear, and I have hardly any thoughts. My body and my emotions feel balanced. I feel a sense of confidence and a stronger connection to myself. It is not that false sense of what we believe confidence should feel like. It is much quieter than that. I feel who I am, and that feels enough. I feel relaxed and completely OK with myself, just the way I am. There is this sense of nothing being stuck any longer. I have this feeling of softness, warmth and flow inside of myself. Everything seems so much simpler, and I know that everything is just the way it should be. It's like everything is in its right place in the universe, and everything will develop and happen at the right time."

I am sure that you can relate to this general description that I have put together from all the different ways I have heard it described. However, everyone's experience is completely unique, so enjoy how it feels to you, in your way.

Congratulations on all the dedication you have given to yourself to reach this stage on your journey to unravelling your focal dystonia.

There are two more stages left.

- Stage 4: Unwinding, resolving and releasing as you develop your extroverted safe state in your nervous system.

- Stage 5: Dissolving the last remnants as you release any residual dystonic movements that might still remain.

However, before we move on to stage 4, we are right now at a consolidation point. It is important for you to continue practicing these three exercises until they are firmly embedded in you. Once again, I advise you to reach out for expert support if you are having difficulty connecting with any of the exercises, or if you notice activation that you are unable to self-regulate when you do them.

This is a similar moment as we had between stage 1 and stage 2. It is best for you to take all the time you need to consolidate these exercises. Rushing on beforehand will not be helpful to your progress. It will only serve to slow you down and create gaps that will later be more difficult to fill.

If you are finding it difficult to slow down and be patient, or if you find that you have a compulsive drive in you that is making you rush on, this is your nervous system in survival mode. Moreover, it is a survival state that you are unable to self-regulate. If this is the case for you, the best thing that you can do for yourself is find an expert therapist to help you to resolve this activation.

I hope that you can really take the time to savour and enjoy this time of deepening and consolidation. It is beautiful and meaningful to do so.

Chapter 13

Stage 4 - Unwinding, Resolving and Releasing

W elcome to stage 4 of your journey. In this stage we will be unwinding, resolving and releasing the survival mode and activation in your nervous system. By the time you have reached the end of this stage, you will be in safe mode and well-being most of the time. Well-being, rather than survival, will have become your default state of being.

If you have been working with a therapist during the previous stages, you will most likely have already been working on the themes of this stage, and you will find this chapter quite familiar.

Know Thyself

Our first focal point is to increase your self-awareness of what is wound tightly within you.

Earlier on in the book, I described the inner experience of survival mode. I also highlighted that we have normalised many of the mental, emotional and physical manifestations of survival mode. You may believe that you are just that way, or it is normal to feel that way, or even not have considered that any other experience is possible. Most critically is when you don't even recognise that it is a survival state. Therefore, you don't realise that your nervous system is activated and the dystonic symptoms are being stimulated and reinforced.

You now have the skill and awareness to debunk this false normalisation within yourself. You now can clearly recognise all your personal activations. What gives you this ability is your skill at being able to drop deeply into the zero-state and the kindness-state. When you are in either of these two states you are in the introverted safe mode that I described at the end of the last chapter. This means that you can now "see inwards" and know exactly what it feels like when your nervous system is in safe mode. From here, you can understand that any other inner experiences that do not feel like this is what survival feels like in your nervous system.

Exercise:

Survival Self-Awareness Exercise part 1

The first exercise in this stage is to become increasingly aware of how survival feels like to you. Before you begin, find a place where you will not be disturbed for about twenty minutes.

1. Connect to your zero-state and allow yourself to deepen into it. Follow the silence inwards, just as far as it takes you.

2. When you are ready, become aware of how this state feels. Become aware of your sense of balance, neutrality

and equanimity. Become aware of the stillness and silence and how there is no sense of rushing nor acceleration. Become aware of your inner connection and of the solidity, confidence and security you feel here; how you just feel "you", nothing more and nothing less, and how that is just simply enough.

3. Spend plenty of time to become highly aware of all these personal experiences.

4. When you feel ready to move on, become lightly aware of all the moments when you don't feel like this. As you do so, become lightly aware of all the inner feelings towards yourself and the world that so frequently accompany you. I say lightly aware because I don't want you to go deeply into them just yet. We will deepen into them to transform and release them in the next exercise. For now, I just would like you to develop your awareness of them.

5. When you feel ready, come back into the zero-state. You can do so with your eyes open and looking at its brainspot, or with them closed. Follow your preference. Once again, feel deeply into the inner sensations and experiences of the zero-state. Finally, at your pace, from there, gradually bring back into your awareness everything that is surrounding you. Do so by awakening your five senses and by connecting to what surrounds you through them. When you are ready, continue with your day.

Exercise:

Survival Self-Awareness Exercise part 2

1. Now go through the same steps, but with your kindness-state. As you become aware of what it feels like on the inside, you will feel how your chest and heart open and expand. You will feel the warmth and softness in your heart and chest. You will notice how your head and mind are soft and sweet. Feel what it is like as these sensations expand into every cell of your body and mind. Then when you are ready, as you did with the zero-state, begin to become aware of all your frequent inner experiences that are different from this kindness-state. Once again, only do so lightly—just enough to recognise them.

2. Finally, as you did previously, when you feel ready, connect back to your kindness-state. Allow yourself to deepen back into it with your eyes open or closed. Feel deeply into the inner sensations and experience the kindness-state. From there, following your own pace and rhythm, gradually connect to your five senses and connect to what surrounds you. Once you feel fully connected to the here and now through your five senses, you are ready to continue with your day.

Let's Deactivate the Survival State

This is the most delicate part of your journey. We will be connecting deeply to the activation in your nervous system, and at the same time, whilst using Brainspotting, we will give your brain the stimulus it needs to unwind, resolve and release it. As it does this, your brain will permanently transform this survival state into safety.

We are going to go at a comfortable pace, always working

within your window of tolerance. Over time, as we continue, your brain will gradually connect to deeper levels of the adverse experiences creating the survival states. Your window of tolerance includes everything that you can self-regulate. If an activation is too strong, that means that you have gone outside of your window of tolerance. As we have already seen, this is a common occurrence for us, as one of the dystonic mental patterns is to be demanding and dissociated. Therefore, it is important to be sensitive, kind and deeply respectful to yourself.

To work within your window of tolerance, you need to be aware of how intense the activation is within you and whether you can self-regulate it. For this to happen, I suggest you go back and read chapter 8 on self-regulation and coregulation. If the activation needs you to be in an attuned relationship for you to regulate, it is essential that you work through this stage of the journey with an expert who has trained with me. You probably have an awareness of the intensity of your activations and ability to self-regulate them, as you lightly connected to them in the Survival Self-Awareness Exercise that we just completed. What did they feel like? Did they feel like they could flare up and consume you? Did they feel like they could hijack you or like you could get lost in them? Did they feel like you could be sucked down into the depths of them? Did they feel like they could shake your foundations? Did you feel like you just couldn't connect or hold on to them and that your mind escaped to somewhere else? If you had any of these or any similar experiences, it is a good indication that you need the attunement of an expert therapist to complete this stage.

If you feel strongly independent and that you want to go through this stage on your own, this is probably an activation in your nervous system. It is a good indication that you need the coregulation of therapy sessions to resolve it.

It is also a sign of wisdom that even though you could work through this stage on your own, you prefer to be accompanied by an expert therapist. There are several advantages in doing so:

- You receive an external perspective that will see connections and aspects of yourself that you are unable to see.
- Even though you can self-regulate the activation, it doesn't mean that you have to. Often, we can process it and resolve it much more quickly in the attuned presence of someone else.
- For most people, focal dystonia has been a very lonely and isolated path. It feels so much better to be accompanied on it rather than continuing on your own.
- Your brain can process through, unwind, resolve and release the activations at a much deeper level and much more quickly in a coregulatory therapeutic relationship. This is because certain centres of your brain are engaged when you are in an attuned relationship. These centres help accelerate your ability to process and regulate the activation.

Whether or not you are working with an expert therapist, there will be some activations that you can work through on your own. In a moment, I will guide you through how to do so. You will be doing a type of Brainspotting that is called self-spotting.

In this specific self-spotting process that we will be using here, there are four brainspots that you can use. They are your:

1. Zero-state brainspot
2. Kindness-state brainspot
3. Resource brainspot
4. Activation brainspot.

In the next pages, I am going to explain each of these brainspots and guide you through four self-spotting processes, one for each of them.

Once you understand how it is to use each type of brainspot, you can begin to use more than one of them to resolve your activations. Each brainspot gives you a slightly different perspective on the activation. It is like an artist who likes to look at what they are about to draw or paint from different angles. They walk right around their subject. This means that whilst they will only draw or paint it from one perspective, they understand it more fully if they have looked at it from several angles. I will explain more about how to do this later on, as you will understand it better after having some experience of self-spotting.

Exercise:

Self-Spotting from Your Zero-State Brainspot

In the previous Survival Self-Awareness Exercise, you became aware of the sensations and experiences you have that are different from how you feel when you are in the zero-state and the kindness-state. Choose one of them to work with. Ideally, it will be one that is with you frequently, if not most of the time. Choose one that, at the same time, is relatively light, that does not feel intense or overwhelming.

When you are ready to begin, find a comfortable place

where you won't be disturbed for about twenty to thirty minutes. You will want to sit in a comfortable chair where your back is supported and where you can sit easily for this length of time. If you would like to listen through headphones to the bilateral sounds, now would be a good time to use them.

1. Begin to centre in and reflect on this activation. Are there any particular life experiences that are related to it? Since when have you felt it? In what situations does it feel worse? In what situations does it feel better? What else comes to mind when you reflect on it. Now go ahead and close your eyes and feel into the activation that you have chosen. Use your interoceptive sensitivity to feel what it feels like on the inside. Where do you feel it in your body? What does it feel like? Does the feeling have an emotional and/or mental tone to it?

2. When you feel as connected as possible to the activation, be aware of how intense it feels. If you were to put its intensity on a scale of 0 to 10, what number would you give it? 0 is that it has completely disappeared and you are in a safe state again, and 10 is the maximum intensity.

3. Open your eyes and look at your zero-state brainspot. Keep feeling into the activation and be aware of the intensity that it has now.

4. As you look at this brainspot, continue to feel interoceptively into as much of the details as possible of what is occurring inside of you. Be aware of the areas of your body that feel in well-being, and at the same time, continue to feel into all the activated sensations.

Simply stay interoceptively present in this way, perhaps for fifteen to twenty minutes, if you can. If you find it difficult, do so for the time that you are able to concentrate.

You may find that the sensations stay the same during this whole time, and you may find that they change and shift. You may also find that they begin to dissipate. Equally, thoughts, memories, images or sounds may spontaneously pop into your mind. Observe everything that happens, just as it is. There is no need to understand anything that is happening, nor to label it or interfere in any way. Just let it unfold and release any need to get involved with it.

We have one simple objective in this exercise. It is to increase your interoceptive awareness of the activation whilst you are looking at the zero-state brainspot. As a secondary benefit, you may find that it begins to dissolve and release. This is a reflection of the natural ability that your brain has to do so, given the right stimulus. However, if you try to make it release, you will interfere with and slow down this natural process.

To enhance the process, we want to focus our attention on the two necessary stimuli. They are:

- Your interoceptive awareness of the inner sensations of the activation and well-being in your body, with as little interference and judgement as possible.
- Looking at the brainspot.

5. When you feel that you are a few minutes away from closing the exercise, begin to add a little bit of awareness of your peripheral vision. Up until now, your gaze has been focused on your brainspot. You will keep it there and at the same time, just add to your awareness a little bit of the blurry images your eyes can pick up on either side, to the left and the right of where you are looking. It is as if you can open your vision outwards a little bit, just adding in as much as you comfortably can.

6. Stay with this for a few minutes more, still keeping yourself interoceptively connected to the sensations that are occurring inside you. When you feel ready to close the exercise, reflect on the intensity of the activation. What number from 0 to 10 would you give it now?

7. To close, you can do like all the previous exercises by waking up your five senses. Through them, become aware of everything that surrounds you, and when you are ready, continue with your day.

As with all the exercises, you want to work within your window of tolerance. If you find that the activation is too strong for you to self-regulate, you are outside of it. At the first sign of this, come out of the exercise and contact an expert therapist to work through it with you.

Whilst our objective is only to increase your interoceptive awareness of the activation, you will find that as you continue through these exercises and over time, this activation will become completely and permanently released. Once that happens, you will find yourself in your zero-state sense of being in this situation in your day-to-day.

Exercise:

Self-Spotting from Your Kindness-State Brainspot

In this exercise, we are going to work with the same activation from a different perspective. Sometimes the activation becomes completely resolved in the previous exercise and the person can no longer find it inside themselves afterwards. If this has happened to you, choose another activation that is similarly light and not too intense.

Go back and follow the exact same steps as you did with the previous exercise, "Self-Spotting from Your Zero-State Brainspot". The only difference is that in step 3, when you open your eyes, you will look at your kindness-state brainspot, rather than the zero-state one.

Work with each of these exercises on a specific activation for at least a week before moving on. You might choose to work for several days with the zero-state brainspot and then several days with the kindness-state one. On the other hand, you might choose to alternate them, using one of them today, the other tomorrow, going back to the first one the following day, and so on.

You are ready to move on to the next exercise, once you have an activation that you have completed these exercises with. By now, the activation is probably mild.

Before I talk you through the next exercise, I would like to give you a bit of technical information about the different types of brainspots.

The first two brainspots we have used, the zero-state and

the kindness-state brainspots, are what we call *expansion brainspots*. This means they connect us to neural networks that are inner strengths and capacities. They are states that expand our capacity to be in well-being. We have an infinity of possible expansion states. For our objective of resolving your focal dystonia, these are the two most powerful ones.

In the rest of this chapter, we will use a resource brainspot and an activation brainspot. These are related to the adverse events you have experienced. In the moment that you experienced this event, part of your nervous system went into survival mode (all the activation that occurred within you, some of which is still stuck in your nervous system). However, other parts of your nervous system stayed very resourceful. These resources enabled you to keep going until the event passed. Without them, you would have simply collapsed. In this exercise, I am going to show you how to connect with these resources. As with all of the exercises in this book, if you find that you can't connect with it, or if it feels too activated for you to self-regulate, you will need to work through it with an expert therapist.

Let's get going.

Exercise:

Self-Spotting from Your Resource Brainspot.

As in the previous exercises, find a quiet and comfortable place where you won't be disturbed and can sit comfortably. If you choose to, use the bilateral sounds. This exercise will take twenty to twenty-five minutes.

1. Begin to centre in on the activation that you have

been working with. Use your interoceptive sensitivity to feel what it now feels like on the inside. Where do you feel it in your body? What does it feel like? Do these physical sensations have an emotional and mental tone to them?

2. Now become aware of where in your body you feel most calm, grounded, centred or peaceful. Even if it is only very slightly, that is enough.

3. Bring your attention to this calmer, more grounded, centred or peaceful part of your body. Feel into these sensations. When you feel sufficiently connected to them, maintain this connection and slowly open your eyes as you do so. You will find that they are looking at a spot that enables you to maintain your connection to these resourceful feelings. This is your resource brainspot for today.

4. Keep your eyes looking at this brainspot and bring your awareness back to the feelings of activation. What do they feel like now? If you were to put their intensity on a scale of 0 to 10, what number would you give it? (Remember, 0 would be that the activation has completely disappeared, and 10 would be the maximum intensity).

5. As you continue to look at this brainspot, feel interoceptively into as much of the details as possible of the sensations that are occurring inside of you. Be aware of the areas of your body that feel in well-being, and at the same time, continue to feel into the sensations of the activation. You want to become as interoceptively

aware as possible of all the details of these sensations. Stay present with yourself in this way, perhaps for fifteen to twenty minutes. If you are unable to concentrate for this length of time, do the exercise for the length of time that works for you.

6. When you feel that you are a few minutes away from closing the exercise, begin to add a little bit of awareness of your peripheral vision. Until now, your gaze has been focused on your brainspot. You will keep it there, and at the same time, just add in a little bit of awareness of what your eyes can pick up on either side, to the left and the right of where you are looking. It is as if you can open your vision outwards a little bit, just adding in as much as you comfortably can.

7. Stay with this for a few minutes more, still keeping yourself interoceptively connected to the sensations occurring inside you. When you feel ready to close the exercise, reflect on the intensity of the activation. What number from 0 to 10 would you give it now?

8. To close, as in all the previous exercises, wake up your five senses. Through them, become aware of everything that surrounds you, and when you are ready, continue with your day.

As I mentioned in the previous exercises in this chapter, the sensations may stay the same for the whole time. Equally, you may find that they change and shift or even begin to diminish. Just follow them wherever they go. There is no need to understand anything, nor to label it. There is nothing for you to do or make happen. Just let everything unfold spontaneously, and stay present, feeling into what is happening with curiosity and complete acceptance. What is occurring is exactly what needs to happen for the massive intelligence of your subcortex to heal your focal dystonia. Remember, the only objective that we have with this exercise is to increase your interoceptive sensitivity of what happens on the inside, having connected to the activation and having brought your eyes to the resource brainspot.

If you wish, you can do this exercise each day. Be open each time to where you feel calm, centred or grounded in your body. It may be the same place each time, or it may change. Likewise, the brainspot may be in the same place each time you do the exercise, or it may be in different places. Your subcortex knows exactly what it needs each day, so trust in what happens.

If you wish to do it some days using the zero-state brainspot or the kindness-state brainspot again, flow with your intuition.

You will be ready to move on to the last exercise in this stage when you feel o activation as you look at the resource brainspot.

If this is your experience, let's move onto the last exercise in this stage.

Exercise:

<u>Self-Spotting from Your Activation Brainspot</u>

This is the brainspot for the neural network that holds the memory of the adverse event and the activation that it has left in your nervous system. This means that frequently, it is difficult to self-regulate the activation from this brainspot. For this reason, we will work with it once there is no longer any activation on your resource brainspot. When this happens, it indicates that you have processed much of the activation, making it much easier to self-regulate it from there. As I frequently mention, sometimes the activation is too strong for you to self-regulate. If this happens, it is essential that you work through it with an expert therapist who can help you coregulate it.

If you are ready to work with the activation brainspot, here are the steps of how to do so.

1. Find a quiet and comfortable place where you won't be disturbed for twenty to twenty-five minutes or so. Sit in a comfortable chair that supports your back well, and if you would like to, put on the bilateral sounds through your headphones.

2. Now begin to feel into the activation. Feel where you notice it in your body and how it feels. Does it have an emotional or mental tone to it? Allow yourself to deepen into your interoceptive sensitivity of the activation. On a scale of 0 to 10, how intense is it? If it has an intensity of 4 or above, go back and repeat the resource brainspot exercise. If it has an intensity of 3 or below, continue to feel into the activation. When you feel significantly connected to it, slowly open your eyes. They will be looking at the brainspot that helps you to connect to those feelings of activation.

3. As you continue to look at this brainspot, feel interoceptively into as much of the details that are occurring inside of you as you can. Be aware of where you feel well-being and where you feel the sensations of the activation, feel into them just the way they are.

4. As you did in the previous exercises, simply stay in this interoceptively sensitive connection, fully

accepting your experience. There is no need to interfere with it. Just be aware of it and follow it wherever it goes. You may experience any combination of physical sensations, memories, thoughts, images, sounds or emotions. Include them all and just observe them. Let them come and let them go without getting involved in them or hijacked by them. Just observe them and experience them with interest.

5. If at any moment all the activation dissolves and you come into complete well-being, you can do what is called in Brainspotting, "squeeze the lemon". To do so, go back to the feeling of activation that you began the exercise with. Do whatever you can to try to reactivate it. Perhaps you can do so by going back to a specific memory or situation that usually provokes the activation. Once you can feel it in your body again, let go of how you reactivated it and come back into the here and now, continuing to interoceptively feel into it. You can repeat this as often as you need to. If you reach a point where you just can't reactivate it in your body, your process with this activation is complete. Spend a few moments enjoying this well-being and when you are ready, skip to step 7.

6. If the activation continues during the last few minutes of the exercise, add some of your peripheral vision as you did in the other exercises in this chapter.

7. When you are ready to finish, begin to awaken your five senses. Through them, gradually come back into the room in the here and now. When you feel fully back, you are ready to continue with your day.

As I said at the beginning of this stage, this is the critical moment your journey. It requires you to take your time to gently work through all the activations that you identified in the Survival Self-Awareness Exercises. Be patient, as it may take you many weeks, or even months, to complete this stage.

Take your time to work through them all. Remember, they are all states you find inside yourself that are different from the sensations that the zero-state and kindness-state create within you. Until now, you may not have labelled them as activations. You may have thought of them as normal and who you are. You may even enjoy them and the false sense of control or strength they give you. You may even believe them to be beneficial to you.

However, the key point is that the safe mode in your nervous system feels like the zero-state and the kindness-state. Anything else is an expression of the survival mode. It is this survival mode that is causing your focal dystonia. Remember, your brain is a genius. This means that as you brainspot the survival states you feel are beneficial to you, your brain will do two things.

First, it will maintain all the positive benefits that this activation brings you. Second, it will find a way of creating the same benefits but without the activation and with your nervous system in safe mode.

As you brainspot these activations and bring them into well-being, you will find yourself responding differently to yourself and others. You will be really pleased about how this feels. You will feel anew, happier, stronger, lighter and more empowered. You are naturally beginning to develop your extroverted safe mode.

By this stage in your journey, you will have become very adept at deepening into your introverted safe mode. This means that when you are on your own, doing the Zero-State and Kindness-State Exercises, you feel profoundly safe. It also means that when you are on your own and connecting to situations or events that were activating for you, they no longer put your nervous system into survival mode. You also now feel safe in relation to them.

Chapter 14

Expand and Strengthen Your Extroverted Safe Mode

Our final step to complete stage 4 is to integrate more fully your extroverted safe mode. You are now familiar with the introverted (seeing inwards) safe mode, meaning in quiet moments with yourself, you are able to connect inwards and feel safety, deactivation and well-being in your nervous system. As you develop your extroverted (seeing outwards) safe mode, you will be able to maintain this level of interoceptive sensitivity and connection to your inner world. At the same time, you will be attuned to what is going on around you and to the people you are with. You can maintain this dual attunement (attuned to yourself and attuned to other people at the same time) all the time, feeling your zero-state and your kindness-state.

You will find that on many occasions, this just naturally and spontaneously happens. We can also learn how to become more skilful and capable of doing so, including in the most challenging of situations.

In this last exercise for stage 4, I am going to guide you through how to do so. You will know that you have completed stage 4 and are ready to move on to the final stage in this journey when you feel you are in an extroverted safe mode, most of the time, during each day.

Before you begin, find a quiet and comfortable place to do this exercise, somewhere where you can sit comfortably for about ten minutes without being disturbed. As you do this exercise, if you wish, you can listen to the bilateral sounds. Choose the situation that you would like to work with. It will be a situation from your day-to-day life that activates you just mildly. Now you are ready to begin.

1. Look at your zero-state brainspot and drop inside yourself into this state. Allow yourself to deepen into it, using your, by now, well-developed interoceptive sensitivity. Spend a few moments feeling all the sensations of this state, physically, mentally and emotionally.

2. When you feel ready, imagine yourself in the situation that you had chosen to work with. Continue to feel inside of yourself and discover what happens as you do so.

3. If you notice that it activates you, let go of thinking about the situation and just stay present with the activation. Feel into all the details of it. Do so just as you did in the exercises in the previous chapter. Once the activation has dropped down to a squeeze lemon zero, you are ready to move on to step 4. Your squeeze lemon zero is when you can imagine yourself in the situation and no activation happens. Now your nervous system feels in safe mode in the situation. This may happen quite quickly, given all the amazing Brainspotting that you have already done. It is also fine if you have to do

the first three steps of this exercise quite a few times over a number of days until you reach squeeze lemon zero. Your brain is going at its perfect pace and needs to take the time it requires.

4. Now that you are at squeeze lemon zero, keep looking at the zero-state brainspot. As you do so, imagine yourself in this situation, attuned to what is going on around you. At the same time, stay inwardly connected and attuned as you maintain your zero-state of being throughout the whole situation. When you are ready to finish the exercise, come back to the here and now by awakening your five senses, as you have been doing in all the exercises.

5. Repeat this exercise each day over as many days as you need to solidly maintain your zero-state throughout the whole exercise. Each time you do it, you may like to gradually make the situation a little more challenging. If this is relevant for this situation, each time, imagine the other person or people saying things or acting in a way that would be a little more activating to you. Imagine yourself, handling it, the whole time aware of maintaining yourself in your zero-state. Over the days, you may find that you can do the whole exercise with great ease and that it only takes you about five minutes to do so.

6. Now it is time to road test what you have been practicing. The next time you are in this situation, be aware of your inner state. To what degree are you able to maintain your zero-state or your kindness-state? What activation is still there? You may find that now there is

no activation at all. If this is the case, simply continue to treat this situation with much awareness. Over time, you will find that you are automatically in well-being when this situation arises and that it requires no more of your attention.

7. If, on the other hand, there is still some activation, work through it using the Brainspotting from Your Resource brainspot and the Brainspotting from Your Activation brainspot exercises. Do so until it reaches a squeeze lemon zero.

8. Repeat this whole exercise using your kindness-state brainspot.

It is called a mental rehearsal when you imagine yourself handling this situation whilst maintaining your zero- and your kindness-state of being. Mental rehearsals are very powerful. We will use more of them in stage 5. In chapter 10 we talked about the myelination process in the brain. I explained that when you repeat something over again, it creates a really strong pathway in your brain. This means that the electrical pulse of the nerves firing will go down this pathway before the weaker ones. Our automatic reactions are our thickly myelinated and strong pathways.

Your brain doesn't know the difference between actually doing something and using your imagination to mentally rehearse doing it. Therefore, if you mentally rehearse handling this situation from your zero-state and your kindness-state, your brain thinks that you really did handle it that way. It will then strengthen the neural network for this.

Susan found tremendous benefit in her daily life with the mental rehearsals. One of the ways that her hyperactive nervous system showed up was in her anger. She described how she would suddenly have anger attacks. She was deeply affected by them because most frequently, it was her children who triggered them. She told me that for the silliest of reasons, she would suddenly become filled with rage. She was eating herself inside with worry of how this was negatively affecting her children, yet at the same time was unable to control it.

Once we began to work together, she understood how the rage stemmed from the adverse events that she had experienced in her early twenties. Using Brainspotting, we deactivated those events in her nervous system. Then I guided her through how to use mental rehearsals to experience herself responding in a different way. She mentally rehearsed being in a typical situation that would trigger her rage. However, she would stay centred in her zero-state and in her kindness-state.

She was delighted with how readily she could afterwards respond in this new and healthy way. To say it lifted a massive weight off her shoulders is an understatement. I think that for her, this transformation was more important than the resolution of her focal hand dystonia.

There are a couple of other interesting observations that are important to make:

- When your brain is given a choice between different reactions, it will choose the one that is most beneficial. Physiologically, it is weakening or disconnecting the neural networks of the least beneficial choices. At the same time, it is strengthening those for the most positive one.
- Looking at the brainspot for this response, whilst mentally rehearsing yourself doing it, accelerates the myelination of its neural network.

To complete stage 4 of your journey, you will repeat this exercise with all the situations in your life that regularly activate you.

You are ready to move on to stage 5 if you can maintain your safe mode of the zero-state and the kindness-state most of the time, day-to-day.

Chapter 15

Stage 5-Dissolving the Last Remnants

B y now, you will have found that, naturally, many of the dystonic tensions in your body have fallen away. This has happened as a result of your healing your dystonic mental patterns and the survival activation in your nervous system. They were caused by the changes in your subcortex made by the adverse events that you experienced. They especially occurred in the limbic system of your brain.

You may find, however, that you still have some dystonic movements. This is because of a part of our brain called the basal ganglia. As I mentioned earlier in the book, it is responsible for making things happen automatically. It is responsible for all our habits, as well as our automatic physical movements, such as the way we walk and our general posture. It has also automated what is left of your dystonic movements.

In this final stage of your journey, I will guide you through four exercises. They will show you how to release these automated dystonic movements and replace them with healthy and fluid ones.

The first step to doing so is to release any asymmetry you may feel in your body.

Exercise:

<u>Coming into Symmetry</u>

You are now familiar with finding a quiet and comfortable place in which to do these exercises and listening to the bilateral sounds through headphones, if that is your preference. You will need about fifteen to twenty minutes to sit comfortably without being disturbed.

1. Bring your eyes to your zero-state brainspot and begin to turn your attention inwards. Feel deeply into all the sensations of this state. Be especially aware of your centre of gravity and of sinking into the central vertical space. This is the vertical space that runs up and down your body. It is the space which is neither the right nor left side of your body, nor the front or the back. It is the space that joins them together. Take a few moments here to deeply feel into all the details of these sensations.

2. Maintain your attention here and keep your eyes looking at the brainspot. At the same time, feel into the general sensations of the right and left side of your body. Notice what you feel. What feels exactly the same on both sides? What feels different on one side from the other? If they both feel exactly the same, feel interoceptively into the sensations of this symmetry. Do so for the time you desire before finishing the exercise.

3. If there are differences between each side, your body feels asymmetrical. Spend about ten minutes feeling into this asymmetry. Inhabit as much of the sensations of the difference as possible. During the past few minutes, as you do this, widen your view a little to include some of your peripheral vision. Do this whilst you continue to look at the brainspot and feel into the asymmetrical sensations.

4. When you are ready to finish the exercise, do so as you are now accustomed to. Come back into the here and now via your five senses.

Over the next few days, we are going to repeat the exercise using three other brainspots. This is how:

Exercise:

Coming into Symmetry Using Your Kindness-State Brainspot

Do the exercise in the same way as you did it, but this time, look at the kindness-state brainspot. Feel into all the sensations that this creates inside you. Be especially aware of the softness, warmth and tenderness you feel. From here, you can observe both sides of your body and continue with the exercise as I described on the previous pages.

Exercise:

Coming into Symmetry Using a Nondystonic Brainspot

Prepare yourself to do the exercise as you have done with the previous ones.

1. When you are ready to begin, close your eyes and feel into the side of your body that is free from dystonia. Feel into the whole of this side of your body. Connect with it and feel into it as deeply as you can.

2. When you are ready, continue to maintain this connection and slowly open your eyes. They will be looking at the brainspot that helps you keep your connection to this side of your body.

3. Keep looking at the brainspot and feel into both sides of your body at the same time. Continue from step 2 of the exercise as I described it previously (Coming into Symmetry Exercise).

Exercise:

Coming into Symmetry Using a Dystonic Brainspot

This is the last brainspot that we will use for this exercise. Once again, prepare yourself to do so in the same way you usually do.

1. When you are ready to begin, close your eyes and feel into the side of your body where you feel the dysto-

nia. Feel into the whole of this side of your body. Connect with it and feel into it as deeply as you can.

2. When you are ready, continue to maintain this connection and slowly open your eyes. They will be looking at the brainspot that helps you keep your connection to this side of your body.

3. Keep looking at the brainspot and feel into both sides of your body at the same time. Continue from step 2 of the exercise as I described it previously (Coming into Symmetry Exercise).

Over the next few days or weeks, you will continue with this Coming into Symmetry Exercise. Do so varying which of the four brainspots you use. You may find that you prefer one of them. If you do, it is fine to use it more frequently. However, do make sure that when you do the exercise, you sometimes use each of the other brainspots.

This is a very interesting exercise to do. Frequently, people tell me that it helps them realise the dystonia wasn't just localised in the one area of their body that was problematic. They realise that they had dystonic tensions or sensations in several other areas of the "dystonic side" of their body.

As you release these sensations, the localised dystonia is becoming less intense. You will be ready to move on to the next exercise when your body feels symmetrical on each and every one of these four brainspots.

Activation from Your Musical Instrument

Your brain works through association. The famous late neuropsychologist Donald Hebb put it like this: "neurones that fire together wire together". Here is an example of what he means. If you had a wonderful time in an event and there was a particular piece of music or song playing at the same time, these two separate things become wired together in your brain. If at another time, even years later, you hear that song or piece of music, all the wonderful feelings of that moment come flooding back.

For many musicians, the same phenomenon has occurred the other way around. Many of us have had painful experiences whilst playing our instrument. They range from being called out or humiliated in front of others to being put under great pressure to play perfectly. This means that for many of us, our instrument has become connected to this pain. The neural networks for the sight, touch or sound of our instrument became wired together with this pain and the survival response that accompanied it.

If you are not a musician, you may have another key object that has this same association. For instance, if you are a writer with writer's cramp, it may be your computer, keyboard, mouse or pen that is wired into your survival state. If you are a sportsperson, it may be the track, the sound of the starter gun, the ball, your racket, golf club, darts, cue and so on.

Depending on your work, you are probably aware of an object that has this association. For ease, I am going to refer to your object as your instrument. Please feel free to replace this word in your mind for your personal object.

Therefore, before we move on, it is important for you to release this "wiring together" between your instrument and the activation. As you do, you will relate to your instrument with your nervous system in safe mode. Here are the steps:

Exercise:

Coming to Peace with Your Instrument

As with all these exercises, prepare yourself to be in a conducive environment and put on the bilateral sounds if you wish to use them. You will need about twenty to twenty-five minutes to complete the exercise.

1. Begin by looking at and then picking up your instrument. At the same time, feel how your body reacts to it. Does any activation occur? If so, where do you feel it in your body? What does it feel like? Does it have an emotional or mental tone? Feel into what you notice. You can do so with your eyes open or closed, whichever works best for you. Now put your instrument down but continue to feel into the activation.

2. You are familiar now with how your eyes will automatically go to the brainspot that most connects you to these feelings. This is your activation brainspot. Take a few moments to look at the brainspot, and at the same time, use your interoceptive sensitivity to feel into and inhabit your body. Feel deeply into the activation, and at the same time, become aware of where your body feels more calm, centred or grounded. On a scale of 0 to 10, how intense is the activation?

3. Remember where this brainspot is. Now close your eyes and feel into the more calm, centred or grounded area of your body. Give yourself a few moments to connect with and inhabit this area of your body. When you are ready, slowly open your eyes and let them go to the brainspot that connects you to these sensations.

This is your resource brainspot for the survival state that is related to your instrument.

4. Keep looking at this resource brainspot at the same time as feeling into both the activation and the well-being. What intensity, on a scale of 0 to 10, does it have now? Stay inhabiting and feeling into these sensations for as long as your time or your concentration permits.

5. A few minutes before you are ready to finish, widen your view a little. You will now be looking at your brainspot, and at the same time, you are aware of some of your peripheral vision. As you do so, keep feeling into the sensations occurring inside of you.

6. When you are ready to finish the exercise, do so in the same way as you are accustomed with the previous exercises.

Over the days and, if necessary, weeks that you practice this exercise, you may like to also use your zero-state or kindness-state brainspot. On the days that you wish, simply feel into the activation, and let your eyes go the brainspot of the state you would like to work with. For the rest of the exercise, you will feel into your inner sensations as I described before. The only thing is that you will be doing this from either one of these brainspots.

Over time, the activation will dissolve down to a squeeze lemon zero on each of these brainspots. Once it has, see if there is still activation on the activation brainspot. If there is, complete the exercise whilst you look at this activation brainspot.

You will know that there is no activation at all with your

instrument when you feel at one with it. It will no longer feel separate or alien to you. It will feel part of who you are. Once this happens, you are ready to move on to our penultimate exercise. In this exercise, we are going to come back to our mental rehearsals to strengthen your nondystonic neural networks.

One of the traps that the dystonia leads us to is to become overly focused on the part of our body where the dystonia is most acute. This is most often the fingers, the embouchure or the neck (in cervical dystonia). This is a trap because we need to have a whole-body relationship to our movements. This is because our movements never come from one specific part of our body. They involve the whole body.

Once again, in this exercise, I am going to refer to your musical instrument. If you are a nonmusician, change this in your mind to what is appropriate for you.

Exercise:

Creating a Dystonia-Free Relationship to Your Instrument

As with all these exercises, prepare yourself adequately to begin. You will need ten to fifteen minutes for this exercise.

1. Look at your zero-state brainspot and lean inwards into all the internal sensations of this state. Feel how all your movements, in reality, initiate from your centre of gravity. Feel how your limbs feel light as they do. Feel how your breath feels free. Feel how your jaw, tongue and face feel relaxed. Feel how everything just feels like it is in the right place. Stay feeling into and inhab-

iting these sensations for as long as you need, until they
feel nicely consolidated.

2. Feel into the nondystonic side of your body and the
fluidity that you feel there. Once again, there is that
sense of everything feeling like it is in just the right
place. You may have a sense of connection and respon-
siveness.

3. If you can remember how you sounded before the
onset of the focal dystonia, allow this sound to come
into your mind as well. It is likely to stimulate your
deep brain to remember how it made those sounds. You
may like to do just these first three steps of this exercise
for several days or even a week before moving on to
include the other steps.

4. When you are ready, imagine how these physical
feelings would translate onto your instrument. Imagine
yourself maintaining your attention in all these physical feelings as you play your instrument and hear the
beautiful sound you make. Avoid the natural temptation of going back to focusing specifically on your
hands or embouchure. Keep your attention in your
centre of gravity and these overall physical feelings of
lightness, grace and fluidity. Feel how balanced your
overall posture is. If you play a wind instrument, feel
how the air flows from your pelvic floor, through your
centre of gravity and right out the end of your instrument in one continuous flow. Feel how your body,
lightly and firmly, forms around it to create a natural
channel for its flow. Spend as long as your time or
concentration permits on this mental rehearsal.

5. When you are ready to finish, come back into the here and now through your five senses.

The next time you practice this exercise, do so looking at your kindness-state brainspot. As you do so, rather than noticing your centre of gravity, you will feel the softness, warmth and tenderness of this state. Feel how it makes your body feel, especially how your legs, shoulders, arms, breath, neck, throat, tongue, jaw and face feel. When you are ready, continue from step 2 as I have just described.

Keep repeating this exercise each day until playing your instrument in your mind in this way feels completely real. You can then include more details about how your fingers, tongue, breath or embouchure feel as you do so. Be careful to keep feeling your whole-body experience as you do.

Once you can mentally rehearse this and have full three-dimensional feelings of it as if it is real, you are ready to move on to chapter 16 and to our last exercise.

Chapter 16

Releasing Any Remaining Dystonic Movements

T his is a truly exciting moment! We are nearly at the end of our journey together. I am so happy for you. You have one last step to take. It is important not to fall into the temptation of rushing this last step. It is important to give your brain all the time and space it needs to complete it. If you pressure yourself, it will only serve to slow down this last step.

Exercise:

Releasing Any Remaining Dystonic Movements

In this exercise, we will use four brainspots. First, I am going to describe how to find each of them. Then I will walk you through how to do the exercise. You will do it using any one of the four brainspots.

Brainspots one and two are your zero-state brainspot and

your kindness-state brainspot. You are now an expert on them, so I don't need to explain how to find them.

Your third brainspot is your activation spot for the dystonic movements. Here is how to find it:

Close your eyes and feel into the dystonic movement. You can probably do so from your body memory of the feeling of it. If not, play your instrument or take the action that provokes it to feel deeply into it. Connect to it and inhabit this feeling. When you are ready, slowly open your eyes so they are looking at the brainspot for this dystonic movement.

Your fourth brainspot is for your freedom of movement. This is how to find this brainspot:

You are now very aware of what the dystonic movement feels like. Now feel into the same area but on the other side of your body. For example, if the dystonic movement is in the middle finger of your right hand, feel into the middle finger of your left hand. Feel into the exact area on your left hand where you feel the dystonia sensations on the right. Feel deeply into this area, and feel its freedom, normality and fluidity. Inhabit these feelings. Then when you are ready, slowly open your eyes so they are looking at this freedom of movement brainspot.

Now you have your four brainspots:

- Zero-state brainspot
- Kindness-state brainspot
- Dystonic movement brainspot
- Fluidity of movement brainspot

The exercise will take you twenty to twenty-five minutes. Prepare yourself as you have done so for all the other exercises.

1. Provoke the dystonic movements either from your body memory or by taking an action that will provoke

it. You want to work off the least activation possible. Your brain will process much better with a lower activation. This means that whilst you can feel the sensations just from your memory, begin there.

2. Now bring your eyes to the brainspot that you wish to use this time. As you look at the brainspot, bring your attention into the here and now. This means that you will be feeling the activation that you are actually feeling in your body right now. Let go of having your attention on anything else. On a scale of 0 to 10, how intense is it?

3. Inhabit these physical sensations, as well as the emotional or mental tone that they may have. Remember, your intention is not to try to make them go away. This will only slow the process down. It is to interoceptively inhabit the sensations down to their finest details, whilst your eyes are looking at the brainspot. From here, let go and trust your deep brain, it knows exactly what to do and the pace at which to do it.

4. Feel the activation and at the same time, feel the ease that you have in the same place on the other side of your body. Feel both sensations at the same time.

5. Begin to include some of your peripheral vision. Feel into these sensations with as much interoceptive sensitivity as possible.

6. At some point today or in the future, the activation will disappear. When they do so, you are ready to squeeze the lemon. Here are the stages:

- Come back to your body memory of the sensations. As they reactivate, feel into them until they disappear once again. When you are unable to find the activation from your memory, go onto the next level:
- Make a movement that creates a small activation. An example might be bringing your instrument up to your mouth or bringing your fingers onto the strings, drumsticks or keys. Once you have created the activation, put your instrument down and brainspot the activation that remains.
- Once there is no activation here, play something simple. Go through the same process until there is no activation.
- Bit by bit, increase the complexity until all the dystonia has completely dissolved.

Be very patient with yourself. Sometimes, these residual movements are stored deep in your brain. When this is the case, it can take a time for your brain to dissolve them.

However, if you are patient and kind with yourself, they will begin to fade away. You may even find that your brain spontaneously remembers how to play in a fluid and free way.

The final resolution to the dystonic movements that Bradley made was beautiful to witness.

He created a dystonia-free relationship to his instrument by paying special interoceptive sensitivity to the position of the muscles on the right side of his face. This was the nondystonic side of his face. In his mind, he heard the beautiful sound that he had been so famous for before the onset of the focal dystonia.

After about a week, he suddenly had a flood of memories about how his embouchure used to feel. They weren't just mental memories. His muscles literally remembered what to do.

He followed this by doing the exercise to release any remaining dystonic movements. They released in a very short time. He told me that in the past, he had never felt very secure about how his embouchure should feel. He said that this was because he had never been consciously aware of it. Therefore, when it failed him with the dystonia, he felt lost and confused and feared that he would never find his good embouchure again.

The development of his interoceptive sensitivity gave him a new and valuable tool. As the body memories flooded back, they were now conscious. This means that he has since refined his embouchure to a higher level than he had before the onset of the dystonia. Of course, he is doing so using his deep brain and the Liberation Model. He is not overly focused on his embouchure and feels it in balance with and relation to the whole of his body. His overall awareness is of his body, embouchure included, forming a gentle but firm channel that surrounds the free flow of air through his body and the instrument. He loves the way that he loses the sense of where he ends and the instrument begins!

Chapter 17
It's Time to Say Goodbye

I t has been an honour to accompany you on this journey. I feel like my part was to be a lantern to guide your way through the darkness that was, for you, focal dystonia.

Now you have come into the light of day, and I am no longer of any service to you.

I have lit your way on a very deep and complex inner journey. It has been a journey with many shadowy corners that you have needed to illuminate and look into. As you have done this, you have become aware of what the focal dystonia has been telling you. As we have made it a welcome guest in your home, it has told you (sometimes consciously and oftentimes subconsciously) about everything that has activated your nervous system and put it into survival mode.

The seventeenth-century Turkish Sufi, Niyazi Misri wrote:

"I was seeking a cure for my trouble;

My trouble became my cure"

As you reflect on this, you can understand the title of this book in a different light. In curing your focal dystonia, through these exercises, your focal dystonia has cured all the experiences that have been afflicting you in so many other ways as well.

They had stopped you from being who you truly are. They had inhibited your creativity and your full potential. They had kept you in suffering rather than being in well-being. They had kept you from your birthright of freely, peacefully and joyfully expressing the full genius of yourself.

My objective was to simplify this journey. I wanted to make it simple without losing its depth and breadth. I wanted to make it accessible and practical, so it can be a functional guide to liberation for you.

I congratulate you for your perseverance and patience. Above all, congratulations for your commitment to yourself. It has brought you to this beautiful freedom.

My deepest desire is for you to feel liberated to express your full creativity. It is that you no longer feel inhibited by the harshness of self-doubt, self-criticism, self-demanding, comparisons or by other people's expectations. It is that you feel liberated to express yourself from the truest and most authentic sense of who you are.

About the Author

Ruth S.L. Chiles has worked with professional musicians, premier and international league sports clubs, and professional dancers, gymnasts, basketball players, skiers and track athletes, enabling them to resolve their focal dystonia and other performance blocks. She has nearly 30 years of formation in and experience with leading edge neuroplasticity and neurogenesis techniques. As a musician herself who suffered and has healed herself from focal embouchure dystonia and other performance blocks, she understands first-hand what it is like to have your deepest passion snatched from you, what focal dystonia feels like from the inside, the experience of the recovery process, and the joy of returning to confident, freedom and fluidity in your playing.

   facebook.com/focaldystoniacure

   youtube.com/FocalDystoniaCure

Acknowledgments

My heart is filled with gratitude to all the people who have been part of the journey that has enabled me to write this book. However, there are a handful of people I would like to specifically thank because of the impact they have had on me professionally or personally.

I would like to begin in chronological order with the great teachers I have been honoured to learn from, then I will give my heartfelt thanks to the people who have touched my life personally.

Firstly, I give my thanks to Erich Schiffmann who taught me about inner stillness as the centre from which all movement flows. I am eternally grateful to Yogi Bhajan for teaching the ancient wisdom and practice of Kundalini Yoga. With you, for the first time my nervous system found a path to peace and well-being. You taught me that my essence is bountiful, beautiful and blissful and that it is worth sharing with the world. Bert Hellinger, thank you for helping me find where I belong and showing me how to create transgenerational order within. David Grand, there are no words to express the magnitude of the gift you have shared with the world in your discovery and development of Brainspotting. Thanks to you I have healed the grinding pain of the trauma I carried inside. I hope to honour you in sharing all I have learned from you with as many people as I can, so they may also be free. Mark Grixti, thank you for giving me a "home" professionally, from which to venture. Your warmth, encouragement and holding is a hearth that fuels me. Mario Salvador and Carmen Cuenca, thank you for your endless service in teaching Brainspotting and the impacts of trauma.

Boo Walker, thanks to your words you move people and open them to new possibilities. Your novels are a gift. I offer you my boundless gratitude for your enthusiasm, feedback and encouragement, which helped me overcome my doubts as a writer, as well as for all your invaluable practical support.

All my love to you both, Rosie and Eddie. You are the reason and joy that carried me through my darkest moments. I am so proud of who you both are.

I am infinitely thankful to the Quevedo Guerrero family, especially to my Custodia. You have made me one of your own and given me a place where I belong. Your warmth, generosity and open arms are an example to us all.

Here in the place of honour, thank you, Levi. I admire you! You are unique in your goodness of heart, responsibility, fun and mischievousness. You are the ground under my feet and the wind beneath my wings.

Printed in Great Britain
by Amazon

84884376R00108